SCHOLASTIC

The Substitute Teacher
RESOURCE
BOOK

GRADES K–2

by Mary Rose

NEW YORK • TORONTO • LONDON • AUCKLAND • SYDNEY
MEXICO CITY • NEW DELHI • HONG KONG • BUENOS AIRES

Teaching *Resources*

To Dot Hanson, MaryAnn Kantu, Susie McGraw, Nell Rogers, Connie Wadsworth, and all the other great substitute teachers it has been my pleasure to know. Thanks for doing a great job in my classroom and in the many classrooms you serve.

Credits: Poems and play reprinted with permission: "The Monkeys and the Crocodile" (page 63) from *Tirra Lirra* by Laura E. Richards. Copyright © 1955 by Laura E. Richards. Reprinted by permission of Little, Brown and Co.; "Not Any More" (page 64) from *Hello Day* by Dorothy Aldis. Copyright (c) 1959 by Dorothy Aldis. Reprinted by permission of G.P. Putnam, a division of Penguin USA Inc.; "Feet" (page 67) from *Whispers and Other Poems* by Myra Cohn Livingston. Copyright © 1958 by Myra Cohn Livingston. Copyright renewed and reserved. Used by permission of Marian Reiner; "Feet" (page 68) from *Everything And Anything* by Dorothy Aldis. Copyright © 1952 by Dorothy Aldis. Reprinted by permission of G.P. Putnam, a division of Penguin USA Inc.; "A Kindness Returned" (pages 69–72) from *Plays Around the Year* (Scholastic) © 1994 by Robin Bernard.

Activities reprinted with permission: pages 61 and 62 from *Play & Learn Language Arts Bingo* © by Rose Orlando and Louise Orlando (Scholastic, 2003), pages 79–82 from *Math Skills Made Fun: Kaleidoscope Math* © Cindi Mitchell and Jim Mitchell (Scholastic, 2001), pages 84 and 85 from *Day-by-Day Math Mats* © Mary Rosenberg (Scholastic, 2002)

Pages: 84 and 85: *Day-by-Day Math Mats* (Scholastic) © 2002 by Mary Rosenberg. Scholastic Inc. grants teachers permission to photocopy the reproducibles from this book for classroom use. No other part of this publication may be reproduced in whole or in part, or stored in a retrieval system, or transmitted in any form or by any means, electronic, mechanical, photocopying, recording, or otherwise, without permission of the publisher. For information regarding permission, write to Scholastic Teaching Resources, 557 Broadway, New York, NY 10012-3999.

Cover design by Maria Lilja
Cover art by Neografika
Interior design by Melinda Belter
Interior illustrations by Melinda Belter (pages 13, 31, and 42), Maxie Chamblis (pages 84 and 85), Jane Dippold (page 83), Milk & Cookies (page 88), Jim Mitchell (pages 79–82), and Mike Moran (pages 19, 20, 24, 59, 60, 63–69, 72, 73, 75, 77, 78, and 89)

1 2 3 4 5 6 7 8 9 10   40   13 12 11 10 09 08 07 06 05

CONTENTS

INTRODUCTION FOR THE CLASSROOM TEACHER

Dear Classroom Teachers,

You may know that for several years I wrote a column in *Instructor* magazine entitled "Ask Mary." It was a "Dear Abby" format in which teachers would ask me questions and I would answer them in the column. One day I got this question from a substitute teacher:

> Dear Mary,
>
> Why do classroom teachers treat substitute teachers so badly? We really feel like second-class citizens, but we perform a valuable service for teachers and for students.

When I read this, I instantly felt a tinge of guilt—not because I have treated my substitutes badly, but because they have been overlooked and underappreciated by our whole profession. So this book is for them, but it is also for you—the classroom teacher. Together we can make the job of the substitute teacher easier and in doing so, help him or her be much more effective in our classrooms.

Giving your substitute clear directions and the tools they need will make his or her day go more smoothly, will offer you peace of mind while you are absent, and most importantly, will assure that your students remain productive while you are gone. But you can do more. Very simply, you can offer the substitute a measure of the respect that they deserve.

This is the answer that I wrote for the "Ask Mary" column:

> Dear Substitute,
>
> You are correct that substitute teachers have not garnered the respect they deserve. Teachers that have spent their career in their own classroom often do not have an appreciation for the difficulties you face every day. So this letter is for all "regular" teachers out there. Please take a moment for some random acts of kindness for these hard-working professionals.
>
> • When you know there is a sub, step into his or her classroom, introduce yourself and say, "Welcome to our school."
>
> • Offer to take any students who are disruptive and to make copies or provide worksheets that might be helpful.
>
> • See if he or she knows where the adult restrooms are and offer to buy some coffee.
>
> • Offer to answer questions about the daily schedule and directions about where to send students for classes such as speech and music.
>
> • At lunchtime, save the sub a seat beside you and make sure he or she is on time to pick up students after lunch.
>
> • After school, thank the sub for being at your school and for doing a great job.
>
> Thanks for all you do for students! —Mary

It is my hope that this book will help you prepare for the substitute and will allow you to work with this person for the best use of instructional time for your students.

Planning in Advance for an Absence . . . You'll Be Glad You Did

Few of the absences you call in will be emergencies—more likely you'll know in advance that you'll need a substitute for a professional development day or a doctor's appointment—and knowing in advance gives you time to develop an effective plan for your substitute and students. As you plan for your absence, think through your substitute's day and try to lay things out in the order in which they will be used. Picture your morning routine and how you automatically reach for lunch count forms and the attendance folder. Then think of the order of subjects that he or she will be expected to teach that day. Leave specific instructions about what children should and should not do, such as, "Use crayons or colored pencils to complete the graph, no markers please." Let the substitute know where you keep supplies in case a child does not have his or her own.

TIP

Keep handy in your personal organizer or address book your district's substitute center phone number and the names and substitute ID numbers of preferred substitutes.

TIP

Show one or two responsible children where you keep your materials for the substitute.

TIP

Contact another teacher at your school and ask him or her to check on the substitute for you. In cases of major or unexpected emergencies, ask this trusted colleague to explain your absence to the students.

Use the checklist on page 6 to help you prepare materials and outline essential procedures. Many of these items should not require much effort on your part, because they may be used on a daily basis. Some items are just for emergencies and a few are essential to make the day go well for both the substitute and for your class.

Substitute-Ready Classroom Checklist

❑ **Class schedule** (reproducible page 9) Make a schedule for the day or week that includes times for announcements, lunch, recess, special classes such as art and music, and so on. If you have this posted in your classroom already, simply let the substitute know where it is. Also include:

  ○ **Clear and complete directions for the day**, listing times that different subjects should be taught, giving directions that explain who does what and when, and telling where to find materials such as answer guides or teacher's editions.

  ○ **A schedule for students with special needs** who will be leaving the room for assistance or receiving help from an aide.

  ○ **A medication schedule**, which shows the time and place to send the child for medication. You might highlight this important information in a bright color.

  Note: If you're using the reproducible on page 9, fill in only the general schedule at the beginning of the year and keep copies on hand to fill in with specific details for each day you're absent.

❑ **Class list** Provide the first and last names of your homeroom students as well as names of students who may enter your room as they change classes for any subject. You can adapt the Multipurpose Chart on page 14 to create a class list with categories that the substitute can check off for great behavior, work turned in, and so on. If you have small groups for reading instruction, be sure to include group lists, too.

❑ **Seating chart** Be sure to include seating charts for your homeroom and for other classes if students change rooms.

❑ **Name tags** These are especially helpful if students do not wear school name tags or if their names are not on desktop stickers. Students can make a stand-up tag out of construction paper or you can provide stick-on name tags. Write these out ahead of time if you can.

❑ **Daily procedures** (reproducible page 10) Explain how you expect the substitute to do the following:

  ○ **Attendance** Give the location of the folder and specific instructions as to how to fill it out.

  ○ **Restroom breaks**

  ○ **Recess**

  ○ **Lunch** Give the location of the lunch count materials and specific instructions as to how to proceed.

  ○ **Dismissal**

❑ **Dismissal procedures and bus information** (reproducible page 11) Let the substitute know who walks, rides a bike, rides in a car, goes to day care or after-school care, and who rides which bus. If you are responsible for taking students to their various destinations after school, include directions for the substitute to do so.

❑ **Class rules and discipline procedures** (reproducible page 13) Explain your management system in detail. The substitute should know what rewards and consequences are appropriate and, if necessary, how to assign points or rewards for behavior.

❑ **Emergency procedures and other helpful information**
(reproducible page 12) Be sure to include information about the following:

  ○ **Directions for fire and tornado drills**
  Directions for these emergencies should be posted in your classroom. Be sure to have your own practice drills near the beginning of school so that students do not have to depend on a substitute teacher to give them instructions.

  ○ **Names of reliable students**
  Let the substitute know which students to call on for help with finding things, bringing materials to the office, and so on.

  ○ **Name and location of a buddy teacher**
  Leave the name of a nearby colleague for the substitute to check in with if he or she has questions or concerns. (Make sure the buddy teacher knows that you have left his or her name as a helper.)

  ○ **Groupings throughout the day**
  Make sure the substitute has updated lists of students who change classes for reading, math, and any other subjects.

❑ **Personal note to students** On the chalkboard or chart paper, write a positive note outlining your expectations to the class. Hang it up after the class has left so they will see it the next morning. Remind them that you will return soon. Include your signature at the bottom. For example,

Good morning, boys and girls! Did you remember that I would be gone today? I will be back in only two more days. I hope you will have a good time while I am gone. Remember to feed the hamsters!

❑ **Helper chart** If you assign jobs for specific students, let the sub know where to find that information.

❑ **Map of the school showing the classroom location** This is available through your school office and is usually posted in your room for fire drill purposes. Make sure the substitute can find it easily.

❑ **Extras** Always leave a few math pages, word games, or brainteasers that the substitute can use if he or she runs out of things to do. If you are reading a chapter book to the class, ask the substitute to continue reading. Leave math or reading flash cards so the substitute can play a quick game and help the students review skills. Keep these "extras" in a box, folder, or drawer clearly marked "SUBSTITUTE." (See page 26 for more on creating a substitute box.)

❑ **Computer information** Do you want students to use computers in your absence? Make your wishes clear and leave detailed instructions if students will be using the computers independently. Do not expect the substitute to be computer-savvy.

❑ **Rules for the playground**
Many schools have more than one playground and specific times that students are allowed to go there. Make this clear to your substitute so there is no doubt about these rules.

❑ **Substitute report form**
(reproducible page 15) Encourage the substitute to fill out the reproducible feedback form to help you plan for your next absence. Be aware that your school may require the substitute to complete a standard form when the day is complete. If that is a requirement, place a copy with the materials for the day.

Tips for Creating a Substitute Folder

Many schools require the classroom teacher to complete a substitute folder that stays on file in the school office. This folder is given to the substitute when he or she arrives. Many of the items listed on previous pages may be included in that folder along with discipline referral forms and a few easy activity papers. See fill-in reproducible forms for creating your own substitute folder on pages 9–15.

To create your own substitute folder, select a folder or binder that has pockets. Then copy and complete the following charts and place them all in the folder. In the pockets, you can put extra lunch-count, attendance, and discipline referral forms and a copy of Discipline Dos and Don'ts, pages 44–47. This way, you can be sure that your substitute will have these essentials without having to look on your desk for them.

Consider purchasing tabs and folder dividers for the folder. Separate the materials into "student information," "schedules and procedures," "emergency information," and "extra activities."

Ask the office to give this to the person who will be your substitute. Be sure to note in your plans for the substitute to return this folder to the office or to leave it on your desk for you when you return.

TIP

Want to be especially nice? Here are a few little things you can do to let your substitutes know how much you appreciate the difficult job that they do:

- Pay for their morning coffee or tea ahead of time.
- Leave stickers or small rewards for them to distribute to students.
- Clean your desk and chalkboard so they start out in a pleasant environment.
- Include name tags for all students.
- Leave a note saying thanks or saying they do not have to grade the papers.
- Ask them what you could have done to make their job easier.
- Buy them a copy of this book!

Class Schedule

SUBSTITUTE FOLDER FORMS

Weekly Schedule

Remember to include times for announcements, recess, restroom breaks, and so on. Use a highlighter to call attention to important details.

Time	Monday	Tuesday	Wednesday	Thursday	Friday

Special Notes About Today's Schedule

Schedule for Students With Special Needs

Name	Needs/Services	Time	Teacher/Room

Medication Schedule

Name	Time	Nurse/Room

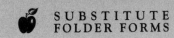

This is the way we handle…

Attendance

_____

_____

_____

_____

Location of attendance folder: _____

_____

_____

Lunch count

_____

_____

_____

Location of lunch cards or tickets: _____

_____

Recess

_____

_____

_____

_____

After school

_____

_____

_____

Hallways

_____

_____

_____

_____

Restroom

_____

_____

_____

_____

Lunch

_____

_____

_____

_____

Dismissal

_____

_____

_____

_____

(See page 11 for a list of students who ride the bus, walk, or are picked up)

Dismissal Time _____

Students Who Ride the Bus

Bus _____

_____

_____

_____

_____

Bus _____

_____

_____

_____

_____

Bus _____

_____

_____

_____

_____

Bus _____

_____

_____

_____

_____

Bus _____

_____

_____

_____

_____

Bus _____

_____

_____

_____

_____

Bus _____

_____

_____

_____

_____

Bus _____

_____

_____

_____

_____

Students Who Walk

Students Who Are Picked Up

Other Notes About After-School Care

People Who Can Help

Reliable Students

_____

_____

_____

Buddy Teacher

_____

Room   Phone Number

_____   _____

School Office Number

_____

Principal's Name

_____

Emergency Procedures

Fire Drill

_____

_____

_____

_____

_____

Weather Disaster

_____

_____

_____

_____

_____

Special Groupings Throughout the Day

_____   _____   _____   _____

_____   _____   _____   _____

_____   _____   _____   _____

_____   _____   _____   _____

Group   **Purpose**   **Time**

_____   _____   _____

_____   _____   _____

_____   _____   _____

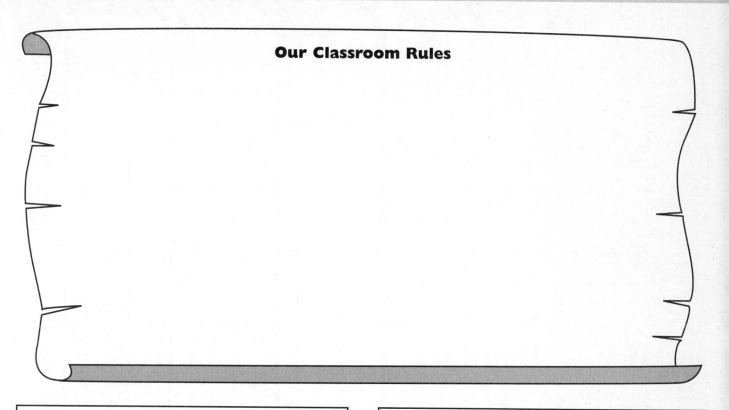

Our Classroom Rules

 Rewards

*When students follow the rules
and are cooperative & productive…*

 Consequences XX

When students break the rules…

Multipurpose Chart

Name

Substitute Teacher Feedback Form

Date _____

Class _____

Name of Substitute Teacher _____

Phone/E-mail _____

	Inadequate/Frustrating	. . . .	Great/Successful
Overall, my day with your class was	1 2	3	4
The lesson plans I found were	1 2	3	4
Our ability to stick to today's schedule was	1 2	3	4
Student behavior and time spent on task was	1 2	3	4

Students who helped _____

_____

Students who worked well _____

_____

Students who had trouble today _____

_____

Student Name   **Action Taken**

_____

_____

_____

Suggestions and Comments

_____

_____

_____

_____

Easy Projects You Can Prepare in Advance of Your Absence

If you know you are going to be absent, set up the substitute day (or days) by starting a couple of projects ahead of time. A little advance planning can assure that the time children spend with a substitute is not just full of busy work, but is organized to contribute to the year-long goals that you have for their learning. Here are some suggestions to follow if you have the luxury of knowing ahead of time that you will be out of the classroom. All of them will leave the substitute with meaningful, quiet, structured activities to present to your class.

TIP

As a general rule, if a substitute is assigned for one or two days he or she should not be required to <u>teach</u> any new material. Substitutes may introduce vocabulary for a reading activity, for example but everything else you leave should be practice on previously covered material.

Reading: *All My Ducks in a Row*

The day before you will be absent, read a story to the class and demonstrate a simple follow-up activity. Give all of the directions and show an example of what the finished product should look like. Then leave the activity for the substitute to complete along with the model. Here are two activity examples that almost every teacher may use without difficulty. If you choose your own follow-up activity, make sure that it is something that requires very little assistance for children to complete.

Activity for The Story About Ping *by Marjorie Flack (Viking, 1983)*

Before you will be absent, read *The Story About Ping*. Show the class the pattern for the duck they will make on the following day when you will be gone. Make a class set of copies of the pattern on page 19 and leave these along with the book for the substitute. Instruct the substitute to have each child color and cut out a different duck. After children have finished coloring and cutting, the substitute can lead a math activity by placing the ducks in single file, two by two, or three by three on the board with sticky tack. Have children practice skip counting to determine the number of ducks that will return to the boat.

When you return, place the ducks on a blue bulletin board with the verse "la, la, la, la, lei." It should appear that all the ducks are lining up in the water to return to their boat (again, you may want to arrange them in a pattern children can recognize). Far off in one corner of the bulletin board, place one duck, Ping. He should be set upside down with his head in the water to show that he does not hear.

Activity for Corduroy *by Don Freeman (Viking, 1968)*

Before you will be absent, read the story *Corduroy*. Leave a class set of copies of the reproducible teddy bear and overalls on page 20 along with the book. Have the substitute distribute the pattern and ask the class what color Corduroy's pants were and what was missing. (Children should remember that his pants were green and that he lost a button.) Then have the substitute give instructions for the children to color, cut, and paste the pants to the bear. When you return, help children "give Corduroy a button" by using a hot glue gun to add a real button to each pair of pants (or the substitute can have children draw on a button). Display the completed bears on a bulletin board. To extend the activity, have children think of things that the little girl and Corduroy did together. Write their stories as they dictate them to you. Display each story under the Corduroy bear.

Reading: *Story Comparison*

If you are uncomfortable with having students cut and paste in your absence, simply leave one or two books for the substitute to read out loud to your class. Copy some of the following questions onto chart paper and instruct the substitute to use it as a guide for discussion following the reading of the story. The questions use standards-based language such as setting and main idea that first and second graders should know. However, slightly easier questions are included in brackets for younger children or those who are not yet familiar with literary elements.

Comprehension Questions to Fit Any Book

1. What is the setting of the story? How do you know that is the setting? [What time did the story happen? Where did it happen?]

2. How would you describe the main character? Why did you choose those particular words? [Is the main character someone you would want for a friend? Why or why not?]

3. What is the main idea of the story or article? Can you explain it to me using only three sentences? [What is the important lesson in this story?]

4. What did you like most about the story?

5. Is there anything that you still don't know or didn't understand?

Reading: *Story Comparison*

Select two stories that compliment each other (perhaps a fiction and nonfiction book on the same topic, two stories by the same author, two stories about the same character, or two stories in the same setting.) Then provide the substitute with the following questions for discussion.

Comprehension Questions to Compare Complementary Books

○ How can you tell that one story is fiction and the other is nonfiction?

○ How are the two main characters alike? How are they different?

○ What tells you that the same person wrote both stories? Are the illustrations done in a similar style? Is the story about the same character or on the same topic? Do you hear some of the same words or language used?

○ The two stories are in the same setting. How are the stories different?

○ The two stories are almost alike. What parts are the same in each story? What is different?

Reading: *Read-Aloud Plays*

The day before you are going to be absent, introduce a play, discuss the setting, and assign parts for the students. Have them read and study their parts as homework. Leave a copy with students' names written by their parts and give the substitute directions to allow students to read the play out loud in class. (See pages 69–72 for a read-aloud play and page 56 for teaching tips to help the substitute.) Read-aloud play collections can match your seasonal themes, for example *25 Just Right Plays for Emergent Readers* by Carol Pugliano-Martin (Scholastic, 1999) and *15 Easy-to-Read Holiday and Seasonal Mini-Book Plays* by Sheryl Ann Crawford and Nancy I. Sanders (Scholastic, 2001).

Name _____ Date _____

Imagine that this duck is one of the ducks from the "Wise Eyed Boat." You choose which duck it is: a brother, sister, aunt, uncle, one of 42 cousins, or Ping!

Color your duck yellow and cut it out.

Name _____ **Date** _____

Do you remember the name of the teddy bear you read about? What color clothes did he wear? What did he lose?

Color the teddy bear brown. Color his clothes green. Cut out both. Then paste the green overalls onto the bear. Your teacher will help you add the lost button

Activity adapted from *15 Easy Lessons that Build Basic Writing Skills in Grades K–2*, by Mary Rose (Scholastic, 2002).

Writing: *All About Me*

The day before you will be absent, give each child a sheet of blank copy paper. Have children fold the paper into fourths and number the boxes. In box 1–4, have the child write his or her name and age. In boxes 2–4, have the child draw a picture of the following: a favorite food (box 2), a favorite outfit (box 3), a favorite game or activity (box 4). If children are able, have them print at least one word to label each box. This page is an organizer for children's All About Me writing, which they'll do with the substitute's guidance.

Collect the completed organizers for the substitute and ask him or her to redistribute the organizers with lined writing paper or copies of page 22 to begin the activity.

Depending on children's writing skills, you may want to leave a class set of copies of page 22 for children to complete with the substitute's help. Or ask the substitute to write the All About Me sentences on the board for children to copy. After writing each sentence, the substitute should pause and help students "fill in the blanks." Encourage the substitute to make sure children use their organizer to help them complete the sentences, matching their words to the illustrations on the previous day's paper. When you return the following day, invite each child to show his or her paper with the illustrations and read the essay out loud to the class. Display the stories and illustrations on a bulletin board. (Alternatively, you may consider asking the substitute to lead the first part of this activity—introducing and drawing the graphic, graphic organizer—and then you can complete the writing above when you return.)

All About Me Organizer

Box 1 name age	Box 2 favorite food
Box 3 favorite outfit	Box 4 favorite game or activity

TIP

First grade children may need for you to write only one or two words at a time—or even one letter at a time—while they copy from the chalkboard. Students in second grade or at the end of first grade should be able to copy complete sentences without assistance and may be able to add another detail sentence about what they like to eat, wear, and play. Guide the substitute to adjust the activity accordingly.

All About Me

Look at your organizer. Fill in the blanks to tell all about YOU.

My name is

I am _____ years old.

I like to eat

I like to wear

I like to play

I think school is

Math and Science Activities

Do not expect the substitute teacher to introduce new math or science concepts. Instead, provide activities, games, or worksheets that reinforce concepts you've taught. When children are already familiar with the material, it is easy for the substitute to review concepts and easy for the children to complete the work. Here are some simple ideas you can prepare in advance.

Hands-On Math

Math manipulatives make great teaching tools, but when you're absent, you may want to steer clear of manipulatives that require sophisticated classroom management skills. Easier manipulatives include a deck of counting cards for sequencing games (see the activity below) or number charts for pattern recognition. (Leave your own activity ideas or a copy of page 76 and copies and an overhead transparency of the 50s chart on page 75. Remember to set up the overhead projector before you leave.)

Counting Cards: Prepare a class set of numbered index cards. Write one number on each card, starting with 1. Number them in sequence so that the number on the last card represents the number of children in your class. Or for children just learning numbers, you may need to make several sets of cards numbered 1–10 (add large dots if a visual representation of the number will help them). Leave the "deck" for the substitute to distribute and use for movement-based counting and sequencing activities like this one: Select half of the class to sit down and the other half to come to the front of the room. Distribute counting cards to the students who are standing. Have this group look at their counting cards and put themselves in order from lowest to highest number and stand in a row as quickly and quietly as they can. Have the "ordered" students hold their cards in front of them. Allow the seated group to verify that their peers are in the correct order. Switch the jobs of each group so that the sitting group has a chance to put themselves in order while the other group sits and verifies. Collect the cards and redistribute them, pass out a different set of numbered cards, or incorporate other appropriate skills such as greatest to least order, odd and even groupings, or skip counting by twos and threes.

Can-Do Science

Treat science in much the same way. Do not expect a substitute to complete complicated science projects. Leave plans for students to read the textbook, answer questions there, or complete some of the reproducible activities provided here (pages 88 and 89). The following object observation activity can also be left for the substitute with minimal instructions. When you return, you can follow up with sorting and classifying activities to do with the objects students used.

Sort-and-Order: This activity is best done with different kinds of buttons, rocks, or seashells. Collect enough of these objects so that every child in the class can have his or her own for the duration of the activity. Have the substitute distribute an object to each student or let students choose from a selection at their table. Then have the substitute model answering the questions on page 24 using an object. If children are able to write, have the substitute distribute copies of page 24 and let the children write their own observations of their own object. If students are not able to write, have the substitute ask one question at a time and have children turn to a partner and share their observations.

Name _____ **Date** _____

Here are the colors I see in my object: _____

_____

My object is about the size of a _____

_____

My object is as heavy as a _____

_____

My object reminds me of a _____

_____

Here is a drawing of my object:

The Substitute Teacher Resource Book • Scholastic Teaching Resources

Worthy Workbook Assignments

Another good practice is to have children tear particular pages out of their workbooks and staple them together. Have them write their names on the top page. Then go over the directions for each page in the packet. Do one or two questions on the most challenging pages and collect the packets. The following day (or days), the substitute can pass out the work and be assured that the class knows what to do.

You can do the same thing in math by creating packets of work for children to complete. The strength of this plan is that students know ahead of time what is expected of them. They will not be able to say that the substitute got confused or they did not know what to do on a certain page. Let children know that you do expect them to finish the work and that it is for a grade—or let them know that there are more pages than they can complete in one or two days and that it is okay if they don't finish but they will have the opportunity to complete it later. This way, you can be sure they will take the assignment seriously.

Test Practice Plans

The day before you are going to be absent, rearrange the children's desks so that they are far apart. Then go over all of the material that will be on an upcoming test. The substitute can administer the test in your absence. It is usually a very quiet activity and if the desks are apart, there is little chance of distractions or cheating. In your plans, remind the substitute to circulate around the room during the test. If you think it is necessary to provide privacy for children while they work, then leave blank folders that can be set up on each desk to shield papers from other students' eyes.

Do not expect your substitute to give performance assessments or any type of local, state, or standardized test. These usually require training so that they will be properly administered. Check with your principal if you know you will be absent on testing days.

Videos With Purpose

If you opt to have the substitute show a video, follow these guidelines:

- Avoid using the video as an entertainment tool to take up time. Planning in advance will provide engaging materials for students to work on and a useful purpose for your substitute (who is not a babysitter!).
- Make sure the content of the video connects with academic subject matter that you're teaching. Can it be followed up with comprehension questions or a critical response assignment?
- Check whether it is legal to show the video. Be aware that it is illegal to rent a video and show it in your classroom. It is also illegal to tape certain shows from your television at home and show them at school.
- Preview the video. Be certain that the movie is free of explicit language, unnecessary violence, religious proselytizing, and sexual content.
- Select a video from your school library. Choose a science or social studies topic or a movie version of a story your students have read. Use the teacher's guide for a follow-up activity or create a page for students to complete after viewing the information. For example, you might have children use a Venn diagram to compare the differences and similarities of the novel and the film that has been adapted from the novel.

Putting It All Together: The Substitute Box

Long before the need arises—as soon as the year begins, if possible—gather a collection of materials that can be used with a substitute teacher. These should be clearly marked "SUBSTITUTE" and can be stored in an expandable folder, a plastic box, or a file-cabinet drawer. Make sure your colleagues and some of your more reliable students know where you keep these materials. You can add to this collection all year long. Just gather extra activity pages, workbook pages, skill sheets, word games, or even craft ideas connected to concepts or skills you've taught. You may need these things in preparation for your own substitute, or you may share it with a substitute who has been called in on an emergency basis for a colleague. Anyone will be able to go to that box and keep children occupied with quality work. This box, coupled with the items on the checklist on pages 6–7 and a couple of projects from the Easy Projects You Can Prepare in Advance of Your Absence section on pages 16–25 will ensure that your class is well provided for even in an emergency.

Important Follow-Up Tips for When You Return

When you return from your absence, you may choose to record grades for the work completed with the substitute. Whether you record the scores or not, be sure to mark each paper that has been completed, even if you put on only a star or a sticker, and hand them back to children. This will let them know that you take this work seriously and may send the message to work even harder for a substitute the next time.

Respond to any notes the substitute has left you, look for a list of children with great behavior (a WOW! List) on the chalkboard and compliment the class on the amount of work they have completed.

Hopefully your substitute was well prepared, his or her day went smoothly, and everyone went home happy. If you do get a report of misbehavior, there are some steps you should take.

1. Find out if a discipline referral was completed.

2. Assess how serious the offense really was. Sometimes children will report things as being terrible and out of hand when really they were just loud because the substitute was there and there was no real offense. Other times they will *not* tell you the whole truth for fear of getting in trouble. If it is not a serious event, let it drop.

TIP

No matter what, avoid group punishments. Remember that no matter what children report, you cannot be absolutely sure what happened in the classroom. It is highly unlikely that **everyone** was misbehaving, so group punishments (and group rewards) are highly unfair.

3. If there was real trouble, allow your principal to handle it.

4. Ask children to brainstorm how the situation could have been avoided. Could you have left more concrete directions? Could they have sought advice from another teacher? Could they have been more kind and helpful? Could they have monitored themselves more effectively? Were they breaking specific school rules? Did they use their best manners?

Preparing for a Long-Term Absence

It is difficult for most teachers to leave their classrooms for extended periods of time. Some careful preparation can make this process easier for you and for your students.

First, be prepared to have another responsible adult in your room and recognize that this person may not teach the same way that you do and will need some personal space and professional respect. Change the message on your school voice mail so that the caller will know that they have reached the person who is your substitute. (A sample message might sound like this: "You have reached the voice mailbox of Mrs. Smith, the current substitute for Mrs. Jones in grade one. Please leave a message.") Put away or take home anything that is really precious to you, so that he or she does not have to be held responsible for your personal possessions. Clear your classroom of clutter to make the substitute's job easier. Clean out your desk, clear off some shelves for him or her to use, and make sure there is space for this person to "move in" and "own" the classroom in your absence.

Second, set some realistic long-term goals that you can expect this person to meet. Look at your yearlong plan and try to gauge what the sub should cover in your absence. You may give specific directions such as, "Complete the reading workbook up to page 56" or "Have children practice writing numerals to 50," or you may just give general directions such as, "Teach this unit on life cycles."

TIP

Some helpful resources that provide structured sequential lessons with reproducible materials or whole-class sets include my books *Week-by-Week Homework for Building Reading Comprehension and Fluency: Grade 1* and *Grades 2–3* (Scholastic, 2002) and weekly magazines such as *Scholastic News,* which also connect students with current events.

Third, try to have your schedule set up so that it is both flexible for the substitute teacher and, at the same time, rigid enough that children can follow a predictable pattern with their responsibilities, homework assignments, and so on. You can make this easier by running off weeks of routine lessons such as spelling or read-aloud homework.

You may want to prepare one hands-on seasonal activity that children can complete and take home some time during your absence. Substitutes do not usually have a file cabinet full of clever ideas and may be reluctant to use materials such as construction paper and glitter unless you have left specific instructions to do so.

Put up a new bulletin board just before you leave so that the sub doesn't have to contend with classroom presentation and decoration during the first week or two.

Fourth, prepare your class. If possible, arrange for them to meet the substitute and get to know him or her at least one day while you are both there. Establish a way to communicate with the class. You might send a weekly e-mail letter, or you could drop your class a quick note during your absence. Be careful that your questions and comments concern the welfare of the children; do not give the impression that you are soliciting children's reactions or checking up on the substitute.

Fifth, plan now for your return by visiting the class just before you come back. You can check the progress of the class and begin to plan the units you will teach next. Be sure to thank the substitute with a small gift or at least a nice note saying you appreciated his or her efforts in your absence.

Evaluating the Substitute's Performance

Let your administrators and colleagues know which substitutes you recommend and which may need extra support when they work at your school. Your principal or another administrator may be able to intervene and help prepare a substitute who is consistently unsuccessful. This form provides a record of your evaluation. Keep a copy for your records.

TIP
Remember to evaluate the quality of the substitute's work—his or her ability to teach and follow the plans in your absence. How much work did students complete and how effectively did they do it? Try not to be overly influenced by stories from students. If you need a gauge, ask colleagues about the substitute's ability to control students in the hallway, at lunch, and at recess.

Substitute Evaluation Form

(to be filled out by the teacher)

School _____

Date of absence _____

Name of classroom teacher _____

Name of substitute teacher _____

The substitute teacher:

	NO	SOMEWHAT	YES
• followed directions for academic instruction.	❏	❏	❏
• controlled the students' behavior.	❏	❏	❏
• left the room neat and orderly.	❏	❏	❏
• arrived and departed at appropriate times.	❏	❏	❏
• completed necessary paperwork in the office.	❏	❏	❏
• handled difficult situations without assistance.	❏	❏	❏

Comments

_____

_____

_____

_____

_____

_____

_____

_____

INTRODUCTION FOR THE SUBSTITUTE TEACHER

Welcome to the dynamic world of the classroom teacher.

The job of the substitute teacher is one of the most challenging jobs in education. It is also one of the most overlooked and underappreciated positions in this country. You are expected to enter a classroom full of unfamiliar students, adapt to specific curriculum and schedules, maintain order, and be on time for everything, and in the case of the youngest children, assume the role of mother or father. Sometimes you will need to deal with children who are grieving for an absent teacher. You may be one of a long parade of substitute teachers they have seen this school year. You may not get a lot of help or respect from the parents or the teachers in the building. You may be called on with the least amount of notice possible. At times it may seem like an impossible task, but with each assignment, you will gain organization and management skills—and confidence. The ideas and guidelines in this section can help you master these skills and make the most of each day in the classroom.

Step One: Before You Set Foot in the Classroom

Invest a couple of dollars in a large tote bag (or invest 25 cents in a paper shopping bag with sturdy handles). Then spend about $5 at your local copy center to buy a package of cheap stick-on name tags and to make some copies of the reproducibles in the back of this book. Select three or four activities and make about 30 copies of each. (Choose a variety of activities—one just for fun, several for reading, one for math, and so on.) You may carry these around for weeks and never use them, but it will be nice to know you have a backup plan if you need something quickly to occupy your charges. If you have a couple of extra dollars, purchase a small package of "good work" stickers. Avoid designs that are seasonal or specific so that you can use them for any grade at any time.

TIP

If you use some of your copies, you may be permitted to make replacements or extras on school copy machines, which are usually in high demand and subject to rules and restrictions. Be sure to ask permission and to copy only to replace what you have used or are planning to use the following day.

Substitute Tote-Bag Checklist

❑ **A copy of this book**
Refer to it for games, read-alouds, or other classroom suggestions.

❑ **Copies of short and easy books that can be read out loud to the class**
(Choose a variety that will be appropriate for different grade levels.
Poetry books are great too. See pages 63–68 for great read-aloud poems.)

❑ **Adhesive name tags**

❑ **"Good work" stickers**

❑ **Copies of activity pages**

❑ **Your lunch**
(Chances are the cafeteria will be serving something you may not want to eat.
Bring your own food and a beverage.)

❑ **Your name tag**
(It is probably required that you wear this when you are on
school grounds.)

❑ **Two or three business-size envelopes**

❑ **Area maps, directions to, and phone numbers of schools in
your district**

❑ **A phone card and some change for emergency calls or a soda
after work**

Dress for a Successful School Day

Remember that in the classroom children will instantly respond to the first impression you give them. Your clothing, hairstyle, and makeup should tell them that you are an adult and that you command their respect. This can be the first step in controlling the behavior of these children.

No one expects teachers to dress like they just walked out of Saks Fifth Avenue, but you do need to be aware that this profession is a conservative one and that parents and other teachers can be very critical of your appearance. Be sure that clothes are business-casual style, provide plenty of coverage, and fit comfortably for all the bending, sitting, walking, and reaching you will be doing in the classroom. Remember . . . if you have to ask yourself if it is appropriate, it probably isn't. *Always* err on the conservative side of this issue.

Step Two: Starting the Day Right

Plan to arrive early and check in at the school office. The secretary will either provide you with a map or show you to your classroom for the day. She may hand you a substitute folder that contains valuable school information, discipline referral slips, clinic passes, and so on. Ask what time you can expect children to arrive in your classroom. This will give you an idea of how much preparation time you have.

You already know that children can be hard on a substitute teacher. They do this because their own daily routine with their teacher has been disrupted and they may be uncomfortable with someone unfamiliar in charge. Further, they may think that having a substitute provides a chance to take a day off from learning or following the rules because substitutes are often not familiar with school or class policies and procedures. You can appear strong and in control if you start the morning in a positive way—and that means *not* relying on students to tell you all of the procedural information.

With each assignment, ask yourself the questions on pages 33–36 and make sure you have the answers to them even before you make a plan for your academic day. Although you may not be able to answer all of these before children arrive, this list will help you get your bearings.

TIP

In the morning, introduce yourself to the principal or assistant principal. You may need his or her help later in the day or you may want to ask him or her for a reference.

Super-Start FAQs

Answers to these questions do vary from school to school. Here are some general guidelines to help you make informed decisions or find the right information. Keep track of different policies at different schools by keeping a copy of School Policy Notes for Substitute Teaching Assignments (page 37) in your tote bag, and filling out the form during each assignment.

What is my role during students' arrival?

Children may wait for you in the hallway or elsewhere in the building. You need to know if and where you need to pick them up. The bells may signal important times in the morning schedule. Find out what time the bells ring and what they signify.

> **TIP**
>
> The very best way to start a child's school day is with a smile, so be sure to greet every child warmly. Nowhere is this more important than in the primary grades, where students are often very attached to their teachers and may be surprised or upset that he or she is gone.

How should I take attendance and the lunch count? Where does it go?

This is one of the most important functions you will do all day. Get it right! Ask the secretary or another teacher to explain how to do this. Children are often assigned to deliver this information to the office for you. Find out who the class "runner" is.

How do I start the school day?

Many schools now have intercom announcements or closed-circuit television announcements. This may include playing the National Anthem and repeating the Pledge of Allegiance. You need to know what to expect and have the students quiet and ready for this. Set a good example by standing quietly for the patriotic observances and listening to the announcements.

What should I do with notes and money and forms that students bring from home?

Children often enter the classroom clutching any number of papers and envelopes containing money. Glance at the notes to see if any of them require immediate action from you or tell you that someone is leaving early or going home a different way. Some schools require these parent notes to go to the office. If not, then be sure to put them in a prominent place so that you remember what to do. Put all official school forms and money in one of the large envelopes from your tote bag, write the classroom teacher's name on the outside, and leave it in a secure place for the teacher or take it to the office when you have a break.

Super-Start FAQs continued

Can I assign students jobs or should I follow the "helper chart"?

The helper chart is a big deal to children. If the teacher has assigned someone to take the attendance and lunch forms to the office or be the line leader, it is very important that you call on that child to continue his or her job instead of randomly choosing someone else. Look around the room to see if helper jobs are posted somewhere and use those names. Being prepared to call on the right helper is one more way that you can give the impression of being in charge.

Where will my students go? What times will they leave and return?

Even if you are the substitute teacher in a kindergarten class, it is unlikely that you will have those 24 students in your care the entire day. There should be a schedule of who goes where and when. Check the schedule left by the teacher or ask another teacher to see if your children will leave the classroom for exceptional education or speech or other classes. Many elementary schools even change classes for reading and math, which means you may work with a new group of students for part of the school day—one more reason to have a stock of those stick-on name tags!

Make sure you know when and where to go for lunch or for special classes like music, art, or physical education.

You may want to write all of these times on the chalkboard or on a piece of paper so that you can refer to it during the day. Children will instantly feel reassured that you are a person who has everything under control.

Do students have names on their desks or name tags to wear as identification?

If you can call a child by name it will help to establish the feeling that you are someone who cares about children in your charge. It can also help with discipline; when children are sure you know their names, they also realize that they are more likely to be held responsible for their behavior. If there is no way for you to know children's names, plan to use your stick-on name tags from your tote bag in one of the following ways:

1. Look in the class roll or attendance book and quickly print the name of each child on a name tag. Pass the name tags out after the morning announcements and ask students to wear them until you learn their names.

2. Put a blank name tag on each desk and ask children to print their names on the tags and stick them on their clothing.

3. Hold the name tags and a marker in your hand. As you call the roll for attendance, print a name on each card and have each child come to you and receive a name tag. As each student gets a tag, say something to each one: "Good morning," "It's nice to see you today," "I'm happy to meet you," "That is a great shirt," "I like the way you have your hair braided," and so forth.

Not only will you have recognized each child individually, but you have started to learn children's names and you have begun your day—and theirs—on a positive note.

Super-Start FAQs continued

How do I manage students' use of the restroom?

To maintain control of the children in your charge, you will need to be cognizant of their whereabouts and behavior even when they leave the classroom. A good rule of thumb is to allow only two children at a time to leave the room for restroom breaks. Even if you have only been with the class a short time, you can probably tell which two should not be out of the room together!

See if the teacher has a policy posted somewhere or if there are restroom passes that children take with them when they leave the room. Ask a nearby teacher about restroom policies. (Do all children go at a designated time of day? Do they go as they change classes from reading or math? How many children are usually allowed in the restroom at a time?) Once again, you want to know the answers before you have to ask any of them.

How do I complete a discipline referral form?

You should complete formal paperwork for any negative behavior that has required more than one verbal reprimand from you or any behavior that has affected the safety of the class, the stability of the learning environment, or the physical facilities where children are located. Any time there is negative physical contact between children or gross disrespect shown to you or another child, you should complete a discipline referral form.

The policy on discipline referrals varies greatly from district to district. After the usual questions that identify the students involved, the form includes spaces for you and for any witnesses to make statements about the events. It is vitally important that you are constantly watching and listening to the children in your control—hence the rules about restrooms! You want to be able to give a clear and accurate account of what transpired. You do not usually name names of other children involved in the altercation. For example, if Mike was pushing Jack, you simply say that Mike pushed another child.

Complete the form, even if you feel the offense may not warrant any action from the principal. The principal can decide the severity of the offense and this will cover you in case there is any legal question about what happened.

What is my role in the dismissal procedure?

Be sure to allow about 10 to 15 minutes for cleaning up materials and packing backpacks before the earliest dismissal. If you are in a kindergarten class, consider having children get ready to leave about 20 minutes early and *then*, when they're all ready, have a story or song time to end the day. This will assure an orderly dismissal for you and for the students. You probably have several hours to worry about this, but it is another critically important procedure for you to do correctly. First, consult your substitute folder and nearby teachers, and then check with children. Find out who rides the bus, who walks home, who goes to after-school care, and who gets picked up by a parent or caretaker. (Filling out a copy of the dismissal procedure form on page 11 can help you keep track of all of this information.) Make sure you know what times to dismiss children and whether you are required to escort them to a certain place. Double-check notes that children have brought to school to be sure they do not indicate a change in after-school plans.

Super-Start FAQs continued

How should I greet the students?

This is where you make that important first impression and it may make your whole day go more easily. Plan to stand at the classroom door and greet students as they enter. Try: "Hi, I'm Mr./Ms./Mrs. _____, and I will be your teacher today. Please enter the room quietly, put your things away, and read the note on the chalkboard." Or, "Hi, I'm Mr./Ms./Mrs. _____, and I will be your teacher today. Please enter the room quietly, put your things away, and complete the paper on your desk." Request that students please hold any money or notes from their parents until after the morning announcements.

Children should enter and hang up backpacks; stow lunch boxes, coats, hats, and so on; and walk to their desks.

What can I expect the classroom teacher to leave for me?

This is a list of what the classroom teacher should have left for you (see also the reproducible substitute folder forms on pages referenced below):

1. A complete schedule for the day, including times for arrival, different subjects, lunch, special classes, recess, and dismissal.
2. Notes about any deviations from the regular schedule, such as school assemblies.
3. A schedule of pull-out programs for students receiving extra support services.
4. Lists of students in instructional groups or students who change classes.
5. Procedures for attendance, lunch, recess, hallways, dismissal, after school, and emergency situations.
6. Notes on classroom rules and behavior expectations, including appropriate consequences and rewards.
7. Attendance, lunch, and discipline-referral forms.
8. A lesson plan for the day.

page 9   *page 10*   *page 11*   *page 12*   *page 13*   *page 15*

School Policy Notes for Substitute Teaching Assignments

Name of School	Grades Taught	Names of Absent Teachers	Procedure Notes	Comments

The Substitute Teacher Resource Book • Scholastic Teaching Resources

Step Three: Implementing Instructional Plans Effectively

Read over the material that explains what children are to be working on for the first hour. Read the answers, too. You want to make sure you're familiar with everything that is presented—even if the material is unfamiliar to you.

1. Print your name on the chalkboard, title first, and stand confidently in front of the room. In a calm, clear voice say, "I am Mr./Ms./Mrs. _____ and I will be your substitute teacher today [or for several days if you know that]. I know that it is difficult to have your teacher away, but we can have a good day if we cooperate and are polite to each other. We will get right to work after the morning announcements." Or "We will get right to work now that the morning announcements are completed."

2. "Before we start reading [or math or another subject], I would like to know each of your names. I will collect lunch money and notes from your parents when I call you. Please work quietly at your desk or read a book at your desk until you hear your name."

3. Pick up the first order of the day as described in the lesson plans left by the teacher. Stand quietly in front of the room and explain what the class will be doing. For example, in a kindergarten class you might say, "Today we will be measuring the height of your bean plants, we will go to art class, and we are going to read about bears. There is pizza for lunch. It is going to be a great day and I am happy to be here with you." You may even want to use the chalkboard and draw a picture of a plant, a paintbrush, a bear, and a pizza. Then you can put a checkmark beside everything as you complete it that day. This helps children to know what is coming next and may alleviate some of their anxiety about having a substitute teacher.

In a first or second grade class, you might begin with the following greeting: "Mr. [or Ms.] _____ has left some wonderful plans for you. I am excited to hear how well you read and to see your writing. I have picked out a special story to read to you and I will take you to recess after lunch. It's going to be a great day!"

Most primary teachers begin the day with some calendar activities or a morning message. Then the students should have some independent work to complete.

Avoid the temptation to interrupt if children are working quietly. Circulate around the room to see that everyone is on task. If you find a student who is not on task, whisper something like one of the following: "I see you need some help getting started." "Do you have a specific question?" "Do you know what to do first?" "Can I help you with this first one?" "Did you understand the directions?"

By using this technique (circulating and whispering), you help students who are having trouble without embarrassing them and you let everyone know that you are watching to see who is working and who is not.

4. Throughout the day, be sure to thank children for working quietly and completing what you asked them to do. Let them know that you will give a good report to their teacher.

5. Continue to follow the teacher's directions as closely as possible. Staying on a predictable schedule makes children comfortable and can actually help with discipline problems. Use a checkmark or star on the substitute plans to indicate things you have completed. Make a note on anything that you had to omit or ran out of time to complete. If there is some down time or you have a few minutes to fill before lunch, try asking some of the trivia questions from pages 59 and 60 of this book or reading some poems found on pages 63–68.

Even the most experienced teachers can misjudge the amount of time it will take children to complete work or how difficult a specific assignment will be. If you find that children complete the work too quickly, use the activity pages in your tote bag. If you find that the work is too difficult and they cannot finish, stay on the time schedule the teacher has suggested. Collect unfinished work and keep it for the teacher to look at and go on to the next subject. On a sticky note, provide some brief notes on each assignment to let the teacher know what areas of difficulty or success children experienced with the particular assignment. This can help the classroom teacher better address particular skill areas when he or she returns. It also helps him or her create more appropriate future lessons for substitute teachers.

No Plans?
Emergency Lessons and Activities

What if I have to substitute teach in an emergency situation? What do I do if there are no plans at all?

If there has been a dire emergency that has pulled the teacher from the classroom, your first obligation is to calm and reassure children that they will be taken care of and that the school day will proceed as normal.

If there has been an accident of some kind, do not give out any information except the most basic facts. Begin in the usual way, "My name is Mr./Ms./Mrs. _____ and I will be your substitute while your teacher, _____, is absent today." Then offer little or no information to the class. If the news is particularly bad, the school principal or guidance counselor will come in and present what they want children to know. It is better for them to get this information from an adult in the school with whom they have an established relationship.

Suggestions of things you might say include:

"Mrs. _____ had to leave school for a little while."

"Mrs. _____ was involved in an accident but I don't have any details. I am sure she would want us to get a lot of work done in her absence."

"Mrs. _____'s husband is sick and she had to leave. I will let you know if I find out when she will return."

"I don't know very many details. I'm sure your principal will be here soon to tell us what has happened."

Your next order of business is to try to make their school day proceed as normally as possible. Decide whether or not to issue name tags. Check the schedule or plan book to see what children are supposed to be doing. If that fails, then offer them an activity page from your tote bag. Do *not* read them funny poems or play comical games to cheer them up. If the situation is really serious, that may upset students.

If children cannot stay on task and insist on talking about the emergency event, pass out some blank paper and suggest that they write a letter or paragraph about the event or illustrate their feelings. If you know the teacher is ill and will not return soon, allow them to make him or her "Get Well" or "We Miss You" cards. Do *not* offer your views about the situation. Avoid saying anything with religious overtones or discussing death and dying. School guidance counselors or trained child psychologists will handle these situations.

Making Your Own Plans

In some nonemergency cases you may be asked to step into a classroom where there are no plans left specifically for a substitute. In this case, you should try to follow the teacher's plan book. You will find that teachers often write in abbreviations, which you may not be able to decipher, and make references you may not understand. Don't panic.

Most teachers have a daily schedule posted somewhere in the classroom. Look around for it and determine what students should be doing at this time of day. If there is no schedule posted, look at previous weeks in the plan book and see if the teacher has listed times that each subject is usually taught. If neither of these yields any information, contact another teacher or reach into that well-stocked tote bag for a fun activity that can occupy students while you get your bearings.

Here is an example of what you might tell your students in this situation:

"Hello, my name is Mr./Ms./Mrs. _____ and I will be your substitute teacher for the rest of the day. I expect you to follow my directions and treat me, your classmates, and yourselves with respect. I will do the same. While I organize some work for you to complete, you may enjoy this activity page I brought for you. You are welcome to color it if we have time."

No-Fail Activities

Here is a list of other things you can ask children to do if you cannot find work for them.

1. Ask students to get a library book out of their desk or from the classroom shelf and read quietly. Permit young readers to read in pairs, especially if they seem upset about the absence.

2. Ask children to give you a tour of their room. Most children love explaining about the helper chart, the hamster, the calendar or the bulletin board. Ask questions even if you know the answer. Compliment them on their good manners, the way they take turns and their knowledge. Comments like, "You have really learned a lot so far this year," will help children feel proud about their accomplishments and focus on learning tasks.

3. Choose a short, engaging book from the teacher's shelf or your tote bag. Pass out drawing paper or have children open to a fresh sheet of notebook paper. Read out loud and while they listen, allow them to illustrate what you read and share their drawings, if they like, when the reading is finished. Discussing the details and story elements (plot, character, setting, theme) is a good way to reinforce what they heard.

4. Pass out 8 x 12-inch sheets of construction paper. Have children fold this in half to make a card or write a letter to the missing teacher.

5. Have each child write his or her name vertically down the side of a sheet of paper. Then help children create acrostics by writing words that describe themselves and start with the letters in their names. If time allows, let them create a self-portrait that illustrates the words they have written. Display these on the chalkboard for the returning teacher to see.

> **Example:**
>
> T—terrific, talented, tennis player
>
> O—outstanding, outgoing, outloud
>
> M—marvelous, melodramatic

Variations on the acrostic:

Have children:
- create a short story, written in such a way that each letter of their name begins a new sentence.
- write complete sentences about themselves, written so that each letter of their name begins a new sentence.
- write the entire alphabet along the left-hand side of a sheet of paper and try to write words that start with each letter of the alphabet. The words should come from categories such as those listed on page 42.

	SEASONAL WORDS	VERBS	SCHOOL WORDS	SPORTS WORDS
A	autumn	act	arithmetic	athlete
B	bob for apples	burst	books	basketball
C	chrysanthemum	cry	cafeteria	coach

6. Almost all children need to work on making their handwriting more legible. Write a paragraph on chart paper or the chalkboard and instruct children to copy it neatly and precisely. Here are a few guidelines.

- Some early third-graders may not yet be familiar with cursive writing. In this case, use manuscript instead of cursive.
- If you sense that children can copy in cursive but need extra guidance, write only one or two words at a time and pause while students copy them.
- Use a midline to show children how to form the letters properly.
- If you can't think of something original, use famous poems or sayings such as Ben Franklin aphorisms—"A penny saved is a penny earned," "When you are good to others, you are best to yourself," and so on.

Step Four: Management Tips to Get You Through the Day

❑ **TIP 1: Be a clock watcher!** The principal and other teachers may not see you working in the classroom, but they will notice if you are late taking your class to other subjects, recess, lunch, or special-area classes. Allow one or two extra minutes for *everything.* Better to arrive early than late.

❑ **Tip 2: Expect to guide students in review work rather than teach new material.** Teachers rarely expect you to introduce new material to the class. Almost every assignment you give will involve skills that children already have acquired. You should not need to review heavily or demonstrate or really "teach" very much unless you are in a long-term assignment.

One exception to this is that the teacher may ask you to introduce vocabulary that is specific to a story or a science or social studies lesson.

❑ **TIP 3: Phrase your questions wisely.** Notice that a wise substitute asks the class specific questions, such as, "Are there any questions *about the assignment*?" Avoid open-ended questions such as "Are there any questions?", which may invite personal questions that you do not want to answer. If that does happen—and children may ask inappropriate questions—just repeat your question with a caveat, "Are there any questions about the directions on this page?" This will defuse the tension very quickly and make a power struggle with the student less likely.

❑ **TIP 4: Make the start of the day count.** You *may* encounter a school where the morning routine is left up to the classroom teacher, meaning that there are no intercom or television announcements. Check the helper chart to see if someone is assigned to lead a song or the Pledge of Allegiance or lead this yourself. Remember that classroom teachers always schedule an opening exercise (or exercises) every morning to signify that the school day has officially begun. It is even more important that *you* open with something that sends this message. If all else fails, work with children to plan out the order of subjects or events for the day or read a poem or story with a message about new beginnings or starting the day, such as Dr. Seuss's *Oh, the Places You'll Go!*

❑ **TIP 5: Know the computer use policy.** If you are only going to be in the classroom for one or two days, avoid turning on the computers unless the teacher has left directions to do so. This policy can help you prevent damage to expensive equipment and difficult time-management situations about children sharing computers.

In some situations children are well prepared to work with computers throughout the day: They have been assigned to turn the equipment off and on and even monitor their own time on the computers. If the policy is clear and children are able to handle this efficiently and automatically, then let them proceed.

TIP

You can maintain order to the last minute of the day by calling children to line up to go home. According to your schedule, you may call walkers only in one group, bus riders together, and so on. This procedure helps you avoid a mad dash as children exit for the day.

DISCIPLINE DOs

Maintain control by directing management questions to the right child and asking discreetly. To avoid asking children questions that may signal your lack of familiarity with procedures and rules ("What time is lunch?" and "Where is the stapler?", call a calm, cooperative child to your desk and quietly ask the question to him or her individually. ("Thanks for coming so quickly, Ruth. Can you tell me where Mrs. ____ keeps her stapler?")

When you are giving instructions, stand firmly in front of the class and speak slowly and clearly. Pass out the papers yourself, or choose someone from the helper chart to assist you.

> **TIP**
>
> Need a helper fast? Choose the child that you think might be a troublemaker. Compliment him on his behavior (he hasn't had time to act up yet!) and ask him to help you distribute papers or supplies or carry something. (Do not send the perceived troublemaker on an errand outside of the classroom.)

Be consistent with everything you say and do. Children will trust and respond positively to teachers who follow through on what they promise (in regard to behavior, privileges, work, breaks, and so on), so you want to only make promises you can keep and then keep all of them!

Wait for silence before you begin talking. This is the number one management blunder for any teacher to avoid: Repeating yourself or yelling to make yourself heard. Say, "Boys and girls, I need your attention, please." Then wait a couple of seconds for them to look at you and get quiet. If this does not happen, stand near students who are still not listening and repeat your request. Use a calm, firm voice. If you are still having difficulty, go to the noisiest group or individual and quietly ask the child or children to please cooperate so that you will not have to fill out any discipline forms today or send anyone to the office. Then repeat your request one more time using a calm, but firm, voice.

While you are getting the attention of the class, do not talk or give directions. Say, "I would like to see your eyes looking at me." When they are looking at you, paying attention and quiet, thank them and give your instructions clearly.

DISCIPLINE DOs continued

TIP

If you are having trouble controlling how much children are talking, reassure them that they will have time to talk at another point in the day. You might hold up a paper that is fun or promise a group activity. Say "I know you want to talk to each other. I will let you work in groups for the next paper (or assignment or activity). Right now, I need you to listen to me." (Or "Right now I need you to work independently without talking to anyone.") If you do say this, make sure you get around to letting them do the activity in which they can talk to others.

Model how to do the work first. Children may need help getting started with their work. Write the first problem, question, or step on the chalkboard and explain it *before* you distribute papers. Even if children know what to do, go over the first two or three steps or problems and call on children to explain what they did, what the answer was, or how they solved the problem. As they begin working, children who understand the task will *usually* be quiet, at least for a moment or two. At that time, say "Thank you for working quietly. This will make a good report to Mrs. _____ [name of teacher or principal]."

Ask for help from your buddy teacher. Most teachers will leave the name of a trusted buddy teacher on whom you can call to help you if things get tough. Do not hesitate to seek help if you are having difficulty. He or she can speak to an unruly child for you, help you complete a discipline referral, or take the unruly student into his or her classroom for a while. Getting assistance is far better than losing control of the class or getting into a power struggle with one or two children. The rest of the class usually breathes a sigh of relief once the disruptive child has been dealt with.

Watch for and acknowledge outstanding behavior. A classic example of mismanagement is that of the teacher who fills the chalkboard with names of children who have misbehaved in class. Turn this negative reinforcement technique around and watch the results. If a child is helpful (running an errand, sitting quietly, listening attentively, being helpful to another student), write his or her name on the chalkboard. Children will immediately ask you why the name is there. Say, "That is to remind me to use this name when I write my great behavior report to your teacher." You may want to be specific in your praise. "She will want to know that Amanda was helpful." "She may want to know that Amanda was kind to Carl." This works *really* well with that challenging child mentioned earlier. Continue to add names all day long. See if you can get every name up there. When the children have left for the day, write the teacher a note on the chalkboard: "Look who was great in class today!" Children will be pleased to see this compliment when they come into class the next morning.

Maintain order and quiet in the hallways. As you line your class up to leave the classroom and enter the hallway, remind them to be quiet and show good hallway manners. While you are walking along, place yourself in about the middle of the line of children so you can see both the front and the back of the line. Usually if you position yourself close to a child who is acting up, he or she will settle down.

If you see someone misbehaving, bring that child to the *front* of the line—avoid sending this student to the back, where he or she is out of your sight and is likely to get into even more trouble. You can also choose to whisper to the child, which helps him or her "save face" in front of the class. Try, "I need you to walk quietly in the hallway right now."

Now that you have read the "DOs" list, take a few minutes to read over the "DON'Ts" list. These suggestions may save you from getting into a difficult social, or even legal, situation in the future.

DISCIPLINE DON'Ts

Avoid trying to "reform" a problem child. You may run across a child whom you think you can help by using strategies to alter their behavior. However, this is not your responsibility nor is it possible to accomplish much in the short time you are with the student. Instead, focus your full attention on the entire class and how the class can work together to accomplish the day's goals.

Never try to diagnose learning or emotional problems. Other teachers and staff see this child every day. While you should report any behaviors you feel the teacher should know about, let the school staff take the lead in these situations.

Never sign legal papers unless you are directed to do so by the principal. All legal documents should be signed by the regular classroom teacher, but if you are a long-term substitute, you may be asked to attend a formal meeting to place a child into or out of a special class. If you are involved in this kind of situation and are required to give your signature, be sure to write "substitute teacher" by your name.

Avoid arguing with the rest of the staff. You may disagree with a policy or philosophy of the school, but keep your opinions to yourself. It is the staff's responsibility to solve their own issues.

Never smoke on school property. If you smoke, find out the rules in your area before you light up. In many states you may not smoke on school property, which might include the parking lot.

DISCIPLINE DON'Ts continued

Avoid taking students anywhere that is not suggested by the regular teacher. Of course this means not leaving the campus, but it also means not eating outside at lunch time or going to the playground when it is not scheduled.

Do not bring a video from home or the rental store to show to the class. In many situations, this is illegal and the content may not be appropriate or grounded in solid academics. Show a video *only* if you are directed to do so by the classroom teacher.

Never administer any kind of medicine. Wash off minor cuts and apply bandages only. Give no medicine of any kind, even topical creams such as sunscreen. Should a child have an allergic reaction, you could be held responsible. Send children with serious cuts, bruises, or bumps to the clinic or school office.

TIP

In the smallest schools where a nurse is not available, the teacher or office staff is allowed to administer daily medications. It is rare that this would be expected of a substitute, but if you are required to do this, be sure to note the time and the dosage. Most large schools will require that students take their medications under the supervision of a qualified nurse.

Avoid giving hard candy. Many schools prohibit giving candy or cookies as a reward for work or behavior, but if the teacher has promised a treat or if you choose to purchase one, be sure to buy individually wrapped, soft, chewable, candy. You do not want to have to administer the Heimlich maneuver if hard candy becomes lodged in a child's throat. Leave gum at home. It is against the rules for students and teachers in most schools.

Avoid making physical contact with children. The most contact permissible is a quick pat on the back. Consider a big smile and a "thumbs up" as encouragement. A kind word or an offer to be the teacher's helper can give comfort and reassurance.

Avoid being alone in a room with a child. Keep your classroom door open at all times if you can, and stay with the entire group of children whenever possible.

Never leave children unsupervised. If you have a problem, call the office for help or find another adult in the building to assist you, but *always* stay with the class to which you are assigned.

End-of-the-Day Checklist

You survived! Now that your day is complete and the students are gone, take a deep breath. Follow this checklist for getting ready to leave for the day:

❑ Clean up the teacher's desk.

❑ Straighten the rows or groups of desks.

❑ Make sure the room is ready for the custodian to clean the floors.

❑ Erase or clean the chalkboard, and generally straighten the classroom (even if it wasn't straight when you walked in!).

❑ Use your own judgment about grading papers. Teachers usually appreciate the effort if you can get it done, especially if you are grading spelling papers, multiple choice, or short-response questions. You should not attempt to score essays, book reports, or long-response written answers. Avoid writing any comments on student papers. It is best to mark the number wrong (e.g., –6) at the top of the page. The teacher can do the scoring and recording while she looks to see what you accomplished.

❑ Leave the teacher a note (see sample below) or fill out a copy of the Substitute Teacher Feedback Form on page 15. She will need to know what difficulties you had, any important announcements she missed, where to find student forms or money, and what you were able to cover.

❑ If you are going to substitute in the same room tomorrow, look over the work that has been left, make any additional copies from this book, and choose a story or poem to read to the class.

❑ If a teacher or principal writes a complimentary note about your performance as a substitute, be sure to save a copy for your files. If you move to a new district, decide to go into teaching full time, or apply for a different kind of job with children, you can include it in your application.

Sample note to the teacher:

Today's date

Dear Ms. _____ ,

Thank you for having me as a substitute in your classroom today. The children were [choose one or two: helpful, cooperative, hardworking, enthusiastic]. Here is a list of the materials we covered [or did not cover]. [Write whichever list is the shortest.]

I hope you will consider recommending me to serve again as a substitute in your building.

Sincerely,

_____

Long-Term Substituting

Most substitute jobs are for only one or two days, but there are many occasions in which substitutes are called upon to teach for a longer period of time. Here are a few suggestions for starting that kind of job.

Before Your Assignment

❑ **If you have the opportunity, spend a day with the classroom teacher.** Here you can observe how the teacher handles routine tasks like attendance, transitions to new activities, and discipline. You should begin your assignment doing things as similar to the regular routine as possible. As you become more comfortable in the classroom, you can make small adjustments, such as what time of day you check assignment books.

❑ **Meet with the classroom teacher and come up with an instructional plan for his or her absence.** For example, if the teacher was going to come back to school after the winter break, you might plan to cover fairy tales and fables in reading, regrouping with addition in math, the unit on the family in social studies, and growing plants from seeds in science.

During Your First Weeks

❑ **Write a letter to parents to introduce yourself.** Be sure to include your school phone number or voice mail number and e-mail address. If possible, set aside one afternoon to meet parents.

❑ **If possible, meet with the other teachers on your grade level.** They will give you guidance about pacing yourself. Don't be shy about asking them for copies of engaging activities they are doing in their classrooms or for suggestions of how to handle your scheduling or discipline. Most teachers are willing to help you out.

❑ **Make an effort to get along with the staff and participate in the school community.** Meet with the principal and offer to serve on a committee; get to know the librarian; take your turn at bus or lunch duty; hold parent conferences; and attend all staff meetings and social functions. When there is another opening at that school, they will be likely to remember your contributions to their staff.

❏ **Keep up with the paperwork.** Finding work unchecked or not graded is a big complaint among teachers returning from an absence. You don't want to leave important work for the last minute, and it is not fair for you to dump it on the returning classroom teacher.

❏ **Save copies of student work.** You can present these in portfolio style at a parent conference and you will have lots to talk about. These papers can also justify any grades you may be putting on report cards and they will be very helpful to the returning teacher.

For particularly poor work, make a copy of the paper before sending it home. Write "Please sign and return" on the top of the page, so you will know the parent saw it. Make an indication in the grade book when these signed papers are returned to you.

❏ **You will need to communicate with parents.** Respond to all non-urgent phone, e-mail, and written messages within 24 hours. Urgent messages about pickup arrangements or conference requests need responses as soon as possible. Schedule parent conferences as needed. You may want to have another teacher, the principal, or a guidance counselor present for the more difficult conferences.

TIP

In some situations, specific adults are the only ones allowed to pick up a child at school. The office will have that legal information on file. Do not hesitate to call them if you have any questions concerning a child's safety.

Preparing to Leave

❑ **Get things back on track.** Near the end of your assignment, begin preparing children for the return of their regular teacher. If you have changed some things in the room, change them back; if you have altered the routine, change it back. This will make the transition smoother for both the returning teacher and students.

❑ **Keep a file folder for each grade level you teach.** Include samples of activities that were particularly successful with this grade level and copies of ideas and activities that other teachers have shared with you. Write yourself notes about what you will do differently the next time you are called upon to be a long-term substitute.

❑ **Remember to thank the principal for hiring you.** He or she may have chosen from among many substitute teachers who requested long-term positions. Your thank-you note may be the key to being asked to return or being recommended for another such job.

❑ **Be aware that students often get attached to their teachers.** That may be the teacher you are replacing or it may be *you*. In either case, the transition from one teacher to another can be very difficult for certain students. Be sensitive to their needs when you first take over and when you are about to leave. Write a note to parents thanking them for their support and complimenting their children. Write a welcome back letter to the returning teacher.

Ideas for Helping Students Communicate With Their Teacher

If the teacher is out for an extended time, consider these suggestions for communicating or welcoming him or her back.

IDEA #1

Cover the chalkboard with a large sheet of bulletin board paper. Let children help you plan a scene that is seasonal, something from a field trip, or a view of the classroom. You (or the art teacher) should make general sketches of the scene in pencil while you plan where things should go. Then allow children to draw themselves in the scene and illustrate the details. Help them write a "Get well soon," "Congratulations," or "We miss you" message. Leave it up for the teacher's return or send it to him or her in the mail.

TIP

You can make student's messages to their absent teacher extra special by adding anything to make the presentation three-dimensional, such as ribbons, raffia string, or glitter. Make the banner a keepsake by having students sign their names and write a short message.

IDEA #2

Distribute sheets of blank white paper and let each child create a page that will eventually be stapled into a book that you can give the teacher. If the teacher is out on maternity leave, let each child write a page of child-rearing advice for the new parents. ("The most important thing about raising kids is . . .") Complete by adding baby-themed decorations such as rattles around the edges of the page.

If the teacher has been ill, let each child write some "get well advice" or an "I miss you because" message. ("To get better fast, I think you should. . ." or "I wish you were back at school because . . .") Allow children to decorate the edges, then staple these into a book with a construction paper cover, and you have a nice keepsake for the returning teacher.

IDEA #3

You may want to consider weekly communication with the absent teacher. You can do this with letters, phone calls, or e-mail. This is particularly valuable if children really love and miss their regular teacher. It helps keep them connected to the teacher they love and can reassure the teacher that all is well in his or her absence.

You'll become a stronger substitute teacher as you gain experience, reflect on your successes and areas of difficulty, and apply the suggestions you have read about. As you learn, take note of the successes you've had each day, and remember that you cannot be expected to do all of these things at once and to be instantly good at all of them—great teaching takes time and lots of practice. If you get discouraged, reread the information in this section and ask yourself what were your strong and weak points—and start over in a new classroom tomorrow. (Those kids have no idea how much experience you have or what you know or do not know!)

Ready-to-Go Activities, Games, Puzzles, and More!

The following activities are designed for use in any situation—some require copying and others do not. They are organized by subjects and skills to help you choose an appropriate activity and report to the teacher exactly what the students worked on. Many of the reproducibles may be read aloud or copied onto chart paper or the chalkboard so the whole class can participate. Or you may want students to complete copies of the reproducible in small groups, in pairs, or individually. For very young or inexperienced students, simply tell the class that you are going to play a question game. Then ask the whole group questions based on the examples on the following activity pages. Young children do not need to score points or be on a team. They just enjoy playing the question-answer game and soaking up the information. (I do not recommend giving prizes for winners, however. Having fun and learning new information is prize enough. If you really want to reward children, reward everyone for playing nicely and cooperating with the group.)

Language Art Reproducibles

To motivate students and encourage them to exercise their language skills, you might introduce a fact, riddle, or poem from this section in the morning and repeat the same information at the end of the day or on a successive day when you are back in that same classroom. See how much information the students can recall.

• NAME THE BABY ANIMAL (PAGE 59)
Children enjoy knowing the names of baby animals. Be sure to complete the examples on this page before you let children work independently or in small groups. Remember that each class will have a wide range of abilities, so consider doing this activity orally as simply a fun exercise (no papers, no competition, no grades) or see the hints below for leading a whole class game.

• NAME THE CHARACTER (PAGE 60)
In this game, children are asked to match main characters to the title of the book in which they appear. This game works particularly well if the classroom has a library or if children can visit the library to find answers to the most difficult questions. This activity is, of course, best done orally with younger students; you could make copies for students in late first grade or second grade.

All of these characters are from books that are considered to be children's classics. Check with the school media specialist to see if you can check out any of these titles and read one or two aloud to your students. If you wish to continue the activity, look through the classroom library or in the basal reader to find the names of additional storybook characters from titles that children have read.

Hints for a whole class game: To make either of the matching activities on pages 59 and 60 a game for the whole class (probably best suited for second grade students), consider dividing the room into halves, thirds, or fourths. As you say one piece of information (such as the name of an adult animal) the group tries to guess the corresponding answer correctly (the name of the baby animal). Allow the group to talk it over and choose *one* group member to respond with the answer. On the chalkboard score one point for each correct answer. The game can be continued later in the day or even on the following day. By conducting the game in this way, you have taken the pressure from any one student who might not be able to respond alone. You can control the noise level by telling the class that you will ask a question to each group on its turn, but if a group misses the answer, the next group will get a chance to try for the answer. Remind groups to hold their discussions to a whisper so that others will not hear their answers.

• LANGUAGE ARTS BINGO (PAGES 61–62)
You can create a Bingo game for children at any stage of literacy. If you are working with a group of emergent readers, for example, you can create alphabet Bingo boards by making 12 copies of the board templates on page 61 and writing the letters of the alphabet in a random order on the boards so that you have 24 different boards. Cut out and laminate the boards so you have a set to reuse. Create a calling card deck by writing each letter of the alphabet on an index card. Keep the cards and boards together in a folder in your tote bag. Other bingo variations for children in grades K–2 include uppercase letters, consonant blends, sight words, word families, compound words, homophones, synonyms (calling cards included on page 62), and antonyms. You can ask a teacher or administrator in your district for word lists at each grade level or get a ready-to-make set for all these topics in *Play & Learn Language Arts Bingo* by Rose Orlando and Louise Orlando (Scholastic, 2003).

To play Synonym Bingo with children at the end of grade 1 and in grade 2, make 12 copies of the Bingo board templates on page 61 and write the synonyms (see the calling card list on page 62) in a random order on the boards so that you have 24 different boards. Or, write the synonym list on the board and have each child copy 16 words in a random order onto a blank board to create his or her own bingo board.

To play the game with a whole class, read the top word from your calling card deck and ask students to find its synonym. For example, *Find the word that means the same as* **large**. Children look for a synonym (in this case, "big") and cover that space with a marker if it appears on their board. Continue calling synonyms until a child fills a row, column, or diagonal line of four answers on his or her board. Have the winner call back the words in the spaces he or she covered and check these against the calling cards you have set aside. Children can trade boards each time they play a new round.

Read-Aloud Poems

• "THE MONKEYS AND THE CROCODILE" (PAGE 63)
Many students are familiar with the poem about 5 little monkeys jumping on the bed. This is an older version that they may enjoy learning and moving to—a great way to motivate children and help them become kinesthetically engaged in their learning. Invite the class to come up with motions or illustrations to fit the poem. Read the poem several times, with four, three, two, and one monkey teasing the crocodile.
(Modern version: *Five little monkeys, jumping on the bed. /One fell off and bumped his head. / He went to the doctor and the doctor said, "That's what you get for jumping on the bed." / Four little monkeys, etc.*)

• "NOT ANY MORE" (PAGE 64)
Teachers often have students respond to poetry by illustrating something in the poem or something the poem makes them think of. This activity helps children build reading comprehension skills. Here is a short read-aloud poem to encourage children to imagine and draw. Distribute copies of the poem activity page or show the poem on chart paper or on the overhead projector. Be sure to read the poem aloud (the class can read along with you) several times to help chil-

dren absorb the rhythm and meaning and to support their reading fluency.

After reading "Not Any More," ask children to think about any toys in the classroom or at their home with which they no longer play. Have them draw a picture of an old favorite and write one sentence about why they like that toy, even if they no longer play with it every day.

• "ANIMAL CRACKERS" AND MY FAVORITE TREAT (PAGES 65–66)
Is it snack time? Ask children about their favorite snacks after you read this poem, which you may want to copy on the chalkboard or use as an overhead transparency. Invite children to illustrate what they would eat for their own "finest of suppers." If children are at the end of first grade or in second grade, distribute copies of both reproducibles, read aloud the poem, and share the "My Favorite Treat" examples on page 66 with the class. Ask children to think of their own favorite treat and draw it on the back of the page. Then have them complete a poetry frame to create their own My Favorite Treat poem. Remind them to look at the model poem and the examples for help: the first line should include the name of the treat and the second line should include a rhyming word that makes sense.
Hint: Remember that almost all poems are better understood with multiple readings. Be sure to read this poem at least three times and discuss what the poem's narrator is saying. For a special touch, purchase animal crackers to serve to the class.

• FEET #1 AND FEET #2 (PAGES 67–68)
Depending on the children's reading and writing level, choose the first (easier) or second (more challenging) poem about feet to read aloud to the class. You may want to copy and distribute the page or show it on the overhead projector. Ask students to help you think of other things that are special about feet. Have them help you write a couple of class poems about feet by creating acrostics. Simply write the letters F, E, E, T, vertically

on the chalkboard or chart paper. Then write either one word that starts with each of those four letters or one phrase or one whole line of the poem. You may want to present these examples for the students:

(Example using one word for each letter)
> **FEET.**
> **F**unny,
> **E**xcited,
> **E**xhausted,
> **T**iny,
> **FEET.**

(Example using a phrase for each letter)
> **FEET**
> **F**lat on the floor,
> **E**xtended over a fence,
> **E**ver wiggly
> **T**rapped in shoes.
> **FEET**.

Read-Aloud Play

• "A KINDNESS RETURNED" (PAGES 69–72)
As a rule, kids love pets and will enjoy this play about three children whose love and care for a neighbor's lost cat is rewarded with the gift of the cat's three kittens. Make a class set of copies of pages 69–72 (pairs of students may also share copies of the play). There are six parts and you can divide the class into six groups, assigning each group to read a part chorally, if you wish to lead a whole-class read-aloud. Or you may want to have each group read the play with individuals taking a role. Props are optional—read-alouds are most often done with students sitting around a circle, reading from their scripts. For an extension activity, ask children to share their thoughts about what animals they think make the best pets. Children should each pick a favorite pet and generate a list describing the pet's attributes. Then ask children to use their list to write advertisements "selling" their classmates on their pets. Younger children can simply draw their "dream" pet and tell the class why this pet is their favorite.

Math Reproducibles

• COUNTING ACTIVITIES: SNOWMAN MATH, MISSING NUMBERS, COUNT-TO-50 CHART (PAGES 73–75)
The first two pages are appropriate for students in grades K and 1 and the third page for students in grades 1 and 2 (and some advanced kindergarten classes). A seemingly simple task for you, children often need practice writing the numerals correctly and placing the numbers 1 to 50 in the correct order.

Before (or instead of) distributing the Count-to-50 Chart, make an overhead transparency of the 50s Chart or copy it on the chalkboard and review it with the class. (It takes only a few minutes to draw the 10 x 5 grid.) Fill in only a few of the numerals, and let students come up and write in some numbers for you. Have one child complete counting by tens; one complete counting in the fifties row and another complete counting in the fives column, for example. When children have completed the Count-to-50 Chart, help them look for number patterns. Here are some suggested patterns: The numbers on the right hand side of the chart are in order by tens. When you look across a row, all of the numbers start with the same numeral. When you look down a row, all of the numbers have the same numeral in the ones place. You can also encourage them to find numbers that are doubles (11, 22, 33, and so on).

• 50S CHART ACTIVITIES (PAGE 76)
Most children need help with basic number sense and one of the best ways of fostering understanding of how numbers work is the use of the One Hundreds Chart. Because this book is intended for younger students, these activities have been adapted for a "50s Chart." Hand out copies of this page to students, review the directions, and challenge them to color in each grid as directed. (This activity usually absorbs children's attention and takes time to complete, which can buy you time to plan your next activity.)
Hint: Run several extra copies! If children "mess up," they may become confused and frustrated and need a new sheet.

- NUMBER HOPPING #1 AND NUMBER HOPPING #2 (PAGES 77–78)

Complete the sample problems as a whole group before allowing children to start on these pages. Children are much more likely to listen if they do not have the paper in front of them as a distraction, so copy the samples onto the chalkboard and go over them before you pass out the papers. To make the page less challenging, ask children to fill in only the next number in the pattern. To make it more challenging, ask children to find the next three numbers in each pattern.

PAGE 79

- KALEIDOSCOPE PATTERNS: GIGGLE BUGS, SPINNING PINWHEELS, FIREWORKS, FLAMINGOS (PAGES 79–82)

Pages 79–80 are geared to children who are just beginning to add and subtract. Pages 81–82 are appropriate for children who can add and subtract two digit numbers (no regrouping is required). On each page, children first solve the problems and then use the color key to determine how to color the designs, which are fun to do and introduce visual pattern concepts such as symmetry. They will need colored pencils or crayons, and a regular pencil.

Hint: Have children cut out their completed kaleidoscope pattern. Collect the pattern pieces to create a colorful display on the chalkboard or wall.

PAGE 80

- THE YO-YO (PAGE 83)

Display the story on an overhead projector or chart paper. Then, read the story aloud together. Invite children to count the coins together and label each one. When children have finished the activity page, have them collaborate to make up their own simple stories and companion math problems.

- MATH MATS: SPORTS TALLY AND AT THE TOY STORE (PAGES 84–85)

These pages help children practice skills as they use clues to determine which kid plays certain sports or buys certain toys.

Introduce one page on the overhead projector and show children how to places Xs in the boxes as they narrow their choices. Distribute the second page for students to do on their own or in pairs. Review the directions with them so they clearly understand the task.

PAGE 81

PAGE 82

Science and Social Studies Reproducibles

The substitute teacher is not usually expected to coordinate science and social studies projects. These activities often take a great deal of planning, require specific materials, and demand excellent classroom control. Here are some simple science and social studies reproducibles that target important learning objectives and can serve you well if you need to teach these subjects.

• MY CLASS AND MY FLAG (PAGES 86–87)
In the earliest grades, social studies begins with a look at the family, then the school, and finally, the community. Here are two social studies pages suitable for grades K, 1, or 2. The first activity asks children to draw a picture of their classroom. Then there are a series of questions for the students to answer. You may need to answer the questions as a whole group lesson if students are not yet capable of reading these independently. You can easily use the data you collect about the classroom (e.g., the number of boys and girls, favorite activities) to make a sticky-note bar graph on chart paper. Each child can place one sticky note in the appropriate column to build the class graph. If children are in second grade, they may be able to make their own graphs using 1-inch graph paper. You will need to set up the graph structure on the board for them.

For the My Flag activity, you may need to use the class flag or a color poster or photograph, if you have one, as a model. This will help children make a connection between the directions and the actual color pattern.

• FACTS ABOUT POPCORN (PAGE 88)
Distribute copies of page 88 or write the facts on the chalkboard or chart paper. Read these facts about popcorn with the class. Stop and discuss each fact after you have read it. Then go back and read each fact a second time so that all students can practice reading the sentences fluently.

If children cannot do the writing on their own, you may want to have the whole class brainstorm some facts they know about popcorn as you write the facts on the chalkboard for children to copy. Then they can either draw a picture of their favorite place to eat popcorn or draw the picture and write a sentence to accompany it. You may want to have children cut out the fact they wrote about popcorn. These make a quick and easy bulletin board display with the words "We learned about popcorn."

• THE AMAZING OCTOPUS (PAGE 89)
Capitalize on children's love of interesting animals with this activity. Before you hand out copies of this page, ask students if they can name some animals that give warning signals. They will probably come up with answers like "Squirrels twitch their tails, birds may have a call, dogs bark, lions roar, skunks spray," and so on. Ask them if they know what an octopus does. They probably will answer that it sprays ink when it's in danger, which confuses an animal that gets too close. Hand out the copies and invite children to read with you about the octopus and its ability to change color when it reacts to different situations. Make sure children have crayons or markers in red, brown, white, and black and ask them to color each octopus to match its feeling. Follow up by asking students whether humans change color depending on our feelings—in fact, we do!

Name the Baby Animal

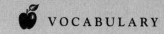

Name _____ **Date** _____

You know that a baby cat is a kitten and a baby dog is a puppy. Can you match the rest of these babies to their "adult" names?

What is the name for a baby . . . ?

1. cow or whale _____

2. frog _____

3. female horse _____

4. goat _____

5. goose _____

6. turkey _____

7. kangaroo _____

8. fox _____

9. bear _____

10. cat _____

11. fish _____

12. eagle _____

13. male horse _____

14. duck _____

15. rabbit _____

duckling

calf   eaglet

joey   gosling

filly   tadpole   kitten

fry   colt   poult

kit   bunny

cub   kid

Name the Character

Name _____ **Date** _____

Draw a line from each character to the title of the book in which he or she appeared.

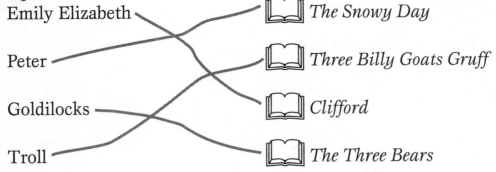

Examples:

Emily Elizabeth   📖 *The Snowy Day*

Peter   📖 *Three Billy Goats Gruff*

Goldilocks   📖 *Clifford*

Troll   📖 *The Three Bears*

1. Viola Swamp   📖 *Green Eggs and Ham*

2. Sam-I-Am   📖 *Strega Nona*

3. Big Anthony   📖 *The Tale of Peter Rabbit*

4. The Man in the Yellow Hat   📖 *Where the Wild Things Are*

5. Max   📖 *Winnie the Pooh*

6. Christopher Robin   📖 *Curious George*

7. Flopsy, Mopsy, and Cottontail   📖 *Miss Nelson Is Missing*

8. Lisa   📖 *Madeline*

9. Miss Clavel   📖 *101 Dalmatians*

10. Cruella DeVille   📖 *A Pocket for Corduroy*

The Substitute Teacher Resource Book • Scholastic Teaching Resources

Play & Learn Language Arts Bingo (Scholastic) © 2003 by Rose Orlando and Louise Orlando.

Synonyms Calling Cards

begin (start)	me (I)	large (big)
unhappy (sad)	beautiful (pretty)	happy (glad)
ocean (sea)	incorrect (wrong)	bunny (rabbit)
bill (beak)	boat (ship)	push (shove)
little (small)	see (look)	fast (quick)

taxi (cab)	under (below)	combine (mix)
writer (author)	toss (throw)	group (bunch)
chair (seat)	difficult (hard)	friend (buddy)
choose (pick)	angry (mad)	fall (autumn)
kid (child)	same (alike)	lots (many)

Play & Learn Language Arts Bingo (Scholastic) © 2003 by Rose Orlando and Louise Orlando.

Name _____ **Date** _____

How can you move as you read this poem to show how the monkeys and the crocodile move and feel?

The Monkeys and the Crocodile

by Laura E. Richards

Five little monkeys
Swinging from a tree;
Teasing Uncle Crocodile,
Merry as can be.
Swinging high, swinging low,
Swinging left and right;
"Dear Uncle Crocodile,
Come and take a bite!"

Five little monkeys
Swinging in the air;
Heads up, tails up,
Little do they care.
Swinging up, swinging down,
Swinging far and near;
"Poor Uncle Crocodile,
Aren't you hungry, dear?"

Four little monkeys
Sitting in the tree;
Heads down, tails down,
    Dreary as can be.
Weeping loud, weeping low,
    Crying to each other:
"Wicked Uncle Crocodile,
    To gobble up our brother!"

Name _____ Date _____

Not Any More
by Dorothy Aldis

I feel very sorry for
Toys not played with any more.
An engine quiet on a shelf,
A dolly sitting by herself.

It must be hard to be a ball
Never thrown or bounced at all.
But lonesomer and still less fun
To be a little top—unspun.

After you listen to or read this poem, think about one of
your favorite old toys. Draw it in the toy box. Then write a
sentence to tell why you really like that toy.

"Not Any More" from Hello Day (Penguin Putnam) © 1959 by Dorothy Aldis.

Name _____   Date _____

Animal Crackers

by Christopher Morley

Animal crackers and cocoa to drink,
This is the finest of suppers, I think
When I'm grown up and can have what I please,
I think I shall always insist upon these.

What do you choose when you're offered a treat?
When Mother says, "What would you like best to eat?"
Is it waffles and syrup, or cinnamon toast?
It's cocoa and animals that I love the most!

The kitchen's the coziest place that I know:
The kettle is singing, the stove is aglow
And there in the twilight, how jolly to see
The cocoa and animals waiting for me.

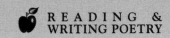
Name _____ **Date** _____

Read or listen to the poem "Animal Crackers." Then read these new "favorite treat" poems.

My Favorite Treat: Pizza & Coke!

Pizza and coke eaten near the old sink
This is the finest of suppers, I think.
When I'm grown up and can have what I please
I think I shall always insist upon these.

My Favorite Treat: Oreos and Milk!

Double stuff Oreos and cold milk to dunk,
This is the finest of suppers, I thunk.*
When I'm grown up and can have what I please
I think I shall always insist upon these.

*Yes, it's okay to use funny words in poems. Poets sometimes make up their own words to make a new sound or to rhyme.

Can you see how the writers used the pattern of "Animal Crackers" but changed the words to write a new poem about their favorite treats? Now, write your own poem about your favorite treat in the spaces below.

Your turn

_____ ,

This is the finest of suppers, I _____ .

When I'm grown up and can have what I please,

I think I shall always insist upon these.

Now draw your favorite treat on the back of this page.

Name _____ **Date** _____

Feet

by Myra Cohn Livingston

Feet are special things
For special kind of fun
On weekdays they walk off to school
Or skip—or hop—or run—
On Saturdays they roller skate
Or bicycle—or hike—
On Sundays they just do the things
That other people like.

Use the letters in the word "feet" to write your own acrostic. Write four words on the lines below. All of the words should describe feet. Be sure to start the word with the letter that is given.

F _____

E _____

E _____

T _____

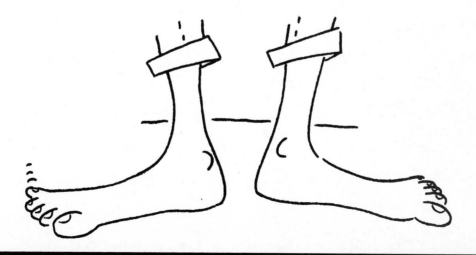

Name _____   Date _____

Feet

by Dorothy Aldis

There are things
Feet know
That hands never will:
The exciting
Pounding feel
Of running down a hill:

The soft cool
Prickliness
When feet are bare
Walking in
The summer grass
To most anywhere;

Or dabbling in
Water all
Slip-sliddering through toes—
(Nicer than
Through fingers though why
No one really knows.)

"Toes, tell my
Fingers," I
Said to them one day,
"Why it's such
Fun just to
Wiggle and play."

How do you feel about your feet? Write your own Feet acrostic poem.
Begin each line of your poem with a letter from the word FEET. Here is
an example with Toes:

Toes

Tap a beat when I hear music
Out they pop from my flip-flops
Ending with toenails
So cute when they wiggle!
　　　TOES!

Feet

F _____

E _____

E _____

T _____

"Feet" from Everything And Anything (Penguin Putnam) © 1952 by Dorothy Aldis

A Kindness Returned

by Robin Bernard

CHARACTERS:
Narrator • Dad • Mom • Pam • Stephanie • Adam

ACT 1

Kitchen of the Williams's home, winter.

Narrator: The Williams have just moved from an apartment into a house. Although moving was a big job, the family is happy to be in their new home and are busy unpacking.

The kitchen door opens and Pam comes in carrying something inside her jacket.

Pam: Look, everybody! Look what I found near the garbage cans! Poor kitty, she's so skinny! Can we keep her, Mom? Can we, Dad?

Dad: Well . . .

Stephanie: *(rushing to look)* She's cold and wet!

Adam: *(rushing to look)* She must be starving!

Pam: And she has no collar!

Children: Please, can we keep her?

Mom: We'll see. But first *(looking at the cat in Pam's arms)* we better get her warm and fed. Here's a towel, Pam. You dry her off while I heat up a saucer of milk.

Stephanie: *(looking in the refrigerator)* I'll find something for her to eat.

Adam: *(grabbing an empty carton)* I'll make a bed for her!

Dad: *(picking up the telephone)* And I better call the police and pound to see if anybody has reported losing a cat.

ACT 2

Two weeks later. The family is at the kitchen table eating dinner.

Stephanie: *(looking into the cat's bed)* Cleo looks so good, Mom. She must like your cooking! Her coat is shiny, and she's not skinny anymore.

Pam: Listen to her purr. She's so happy here!

Adam: *(speaking to his father)* We are going to keep her, Dad, aren't we?

Dad: Probably Adam, but we can't be sure for another few days. If nobody answers the ad we put in the newspaper, Cleo will definitely belong to us.

The Substitute Teacher Resource Book • Scholastic Teaching Resources

*As Pam gets up to put her plate in the sink, the telephone rings.
She answers it.*

Pam: *(dropping the phone receiver and running out of the room crying)*
No! It's not fair! Cleo is OUR cat!

Stephanie and Adam hurry after Pam.

ACT 3

Later, the same night.

Adam: But I don't want to give Cleo away! How do we know they'll
take good care of her?

Stephanie: How do we know they'll feed her enough?

Pam: How do we know they'll love her as much as we do?

Mom: All of you—just listen. The Nelsons moved here just a week
before we did and Muffin—our Cleo—got lost the very first day.
That's why she was so skinny when Pam found her. And their
little girl has been crying ever since because she misses her cat
so much. Just try to imagine how she feels.

Pam: We don't have to imagine, Mom. We'll feel just as bad when
they come to take her back.

Dad: I know it hurts to give up Cleo, but she belongs to the Nelsons.
They've been worried sick about her, and were afraid they
might never see her again. We have to give Cleo back to her
family; that's where she belongs.

The children sadly nod their heads and leave the room looking miserable.

ACT 4

Two months later. Mrs. Williams is looking out of the kitchen window. The children come in carrying their school books and lunch boxes.

Mom: Don't take your coats off, kids. We have a party to go to.

Adam: A party?

Stephanie: Whose party?

Pam: Is it a birthday party?

Mom: Yes—and it's for triplets!

Children: Triplets?!

Mom: Well, furry triplets. Mrs. Nelson called this morning to thank all of you. She said if you hadn't taken such good care of Muffin, she never would have had such healthy kittens!

Children: Kittens!?

Mom: Three of them . . . six weeks old today, and there's one for each of you!

The children laugh and cheer, and rush out the door with their mother.

The Substitute Teacher Resource Book • Scholastic Teaching Resources

Snowman Math

Name _____   Date _____

The number on the hat of each snowman tells you how many buttons he should have. First trace the number. Then draw on the correct number of buttons for each snowman. Then decorate each snowman any way you like.

The Substitute Teacher Resource Book • Scholastic Teaching Resources

Missing Numbers

Name _____ **Date** _____

Directions: Fill in the missing numbers.

Name _____ **Date** _____

Look on this chart and find number one.
In the box beside of it, write number two.
In the next box, write a number three.
Keep going until you get to the end of the row.
Then start with 6 in the next row and keep counting until
you get to 50. Some of the numbers are there to help you.

1	2			
6				
16				
	27			
		38		
41				

50s Chart Activities

Name _____ **Date** _____

1. Color all of the numerals that contain a 6. Circle every numeral that is a double, like 22.

1	2	3	4	5
6	7	8	9	10
11	12	13	14	15
16	17	18	19	20
21	22	23	24	25
26	27	28	29	30
31	32	33	34	35
36	37	38	39	40
41	42	43	44	45
46	47	48	49	50

2. Start at number one and color every number you say when you are counting by fives.

1	2	3	4	5
6	7	8	9	10
11	12	13	14	15
16	17	18	19	20
21	22	23	24	25
26	27	28	29	30
31	32	33	34	35
36	37	38	39	40
41	42	43	44	45
46	47	48	49	50

3. Color all of the numbers that contain a zero. Change colors when you get to 30.

1	2	3	4	5
6	7	8	9	10
11	12	13	14	15
16	17	18	19	20
21	22	23	24	25
26	27	28	29	30
31	32	33	34	35
36	37	38	39	40
41	42	43	44	45
46	47	48	49	50

4. Start at 2 and color every number you say when you are counting by twos.

1	2	3	4	5
6	7	8	9	10
11	12	13	14	15
16	17	18	19	20
21	22	23	24	25
26	27	28	29	30
31	32	33	34	35
36	37	38	39	40
41	42	43	44	45
46	47	48	49	50

The Substitute Teacher Resource Book • Scholastic Teaching Resources

Name _____ Date _____

Help the frog get to his supper by completing these patterns.

Example:

2   4   6   8   10   12

Now try these by yourself.

15   16   17   ___   ___   ___

3   6   ___   ___   15   ___

4   8   ___   16   ___   ___

5   10   15   ___   ___   ___

10   20   ___   ___   50   ___

20   22   ___   26   ___   ___

Use a number line to help you!

1	2	3	4	5	6	7	8	9	10	11	12	13	14	15
16	17	18	19	20	21	22	23	24	25	26	27	28	29	30
31	32	33	34	35	36	37	38	39	40	41	42	43	44	45
46	47	48	49	50	51	52	53	54	55	56	57	58	59	60

Number Hopping #2

Name _____ **Date** _____

Help the rabbit get her carrot by completing these patterns.

Example:

10 20 30 40 50 60 70

Now try these by yourself.

12 14 16 ___ ___ ___ ___

5 6 7 ___ ___ ___ ___

11 22 33 ___ ___ ___ ___

These are a little tougher! Check the example!

Example:

99 98 97 96 95 94 93

Now try these for yourself.

20 18 16 14 ___ ___ ___

70 60 50 ___ ___ ___ ___

30 25 20 ___ ___ ___ ___

Use a number line to help you!

1	2	3	4	5	6	7	8	9	10	11	12	13	14	15
16	17	18	19	20	21	22	23	24	25	26	27	28	29	30
31	32	33	34	35	36	37	38	39	40	41	42	43	44	45
46	47	48	49	50	51	52	53	54	55	56	57	58	59	60
61	62	63	64	65	66	67	68	69	70	71	72	73	74	75

The Substitute Teacher Resource Book • Scholastic Teaching Resources

Name _____ **Date** _____

Solve the problems.

If the answer is		Color the shape
1, 2, 3, or 4	➡	yellow
5, 6, 7, or 8	➡	orange
9, 10, 11, or 12	➡	green

Fill in the other shapes with colors of your choice.

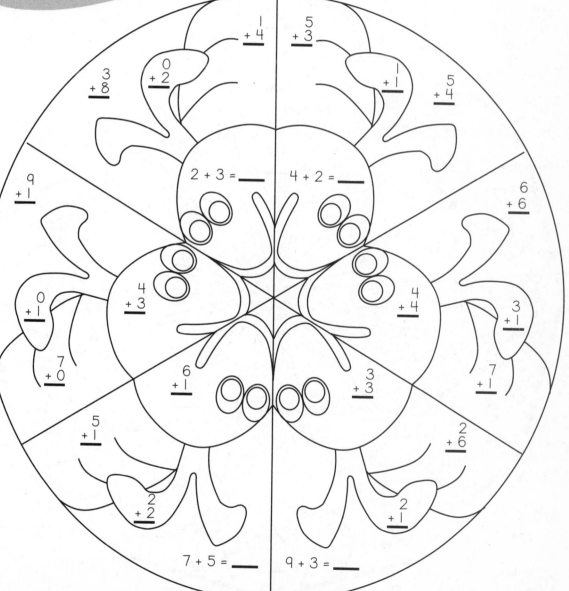

Math Skills Made Fun: Kaleidoscope Math (Scholastic) © 2001 by Cindi Mitchell and Jim Mitchell.

Name _____   **Date** _____

Solve the problems.

If the answer is		Color the shape
1, 2, 3, or 4	⟶	blue
5, 6, 7, or 8	⟶	red
9, 10, 11, or 12	⟶	yellow

Fill in the other shapes with colors of your choice.

$$\begin{array}{r} 9 \\ -1 \\ \hline \end{array}$$

$$\begin{array}{r} 12 \\ -9 \\ \hline \end{array} \qquad \begin{array}{r} 12 \\ -0 \\ \hline \end{array} \qquad \begin{array}{r} 7 \\ -1 \\ \hline \end{array} \qquad \begin{array}{r} 12 \\ -8 \\ \hline \end{array} \qquad \begin{array}{r} 12 \\ -3 \\ \hline \end{array}$$

$10 - 6 = \underline{\quad}$ $\qquad$ $12 - 1 = \underline{\quad}$

$12 - 7 = \underline{\quad}$ $\qquad$ $10 - 5 = \underline{\quad}$

$10 - 1 = \underline{\quad}$ $\qquad$ $11 - 9 = \underline{\quad}$

$$\begin{array}{r} 12 \\ -2 \\ \hline \end{array} \qquad \begin{array}{r} 12 \\ -8 \\ \hline \end{array} \qquad \begin{array}{r} 11 \\ -6 \\ \hline \end{array} \qquad \begin{array}{r} 11 \\ -2 \\ \hline \end{array} \qquad \begin{array}{r} 12 \\ -10 \\ \hline \end{array}$$

$$\begin{array}{r} 9 \\ -3 \\ \hline \end{array}$$

The Substitute Teacher Resource Book • Scholastic Teaching Resources

Fireworks

Name _____ Date _____

Solve the problems.

Fill in the other shapes with colors of your choice.

If the answer is between		Color the shape
1 and 30	➔	yellow
31 and 60	➔	blue
61 and 100	➔	orange

18 + 21

64 + 34

26 + 21

24 + 32

42 + 23

21 + 27

13 + 33

20 + 30

12 + 11

14 + 13

41 + 58 = ___

34 + 34 = ___

21 + 72 = ___

41 + 32

22 + 23

47 + 50

21 + 33

32 + 26

34 + 23

33 + 20

30 + 24

18 + 10

12 + 12

21 + 56 = ___

42 + 46 = ___

31 + 60 = ___

10 + 32

37 + 51

53 + 46

29 + 20

41 + 12

25 + 31

21 + 31

22 + 33

Math Skills Made Fun: Kaleidoscope Math (Scholastic) © 2001 by Cindi Mitchell and Jim Mitchell.

The Substitute Teacher Resource Book • Scholastic Teaching Resources

Name _____ **Date** _____

Solve the problems.

If the answer is between		Color the shape
1 and 30	➝	purple
31 and 60	➝	yellow
61 and 100	➝	blue

Fill in the other shapes with colors of your choice.

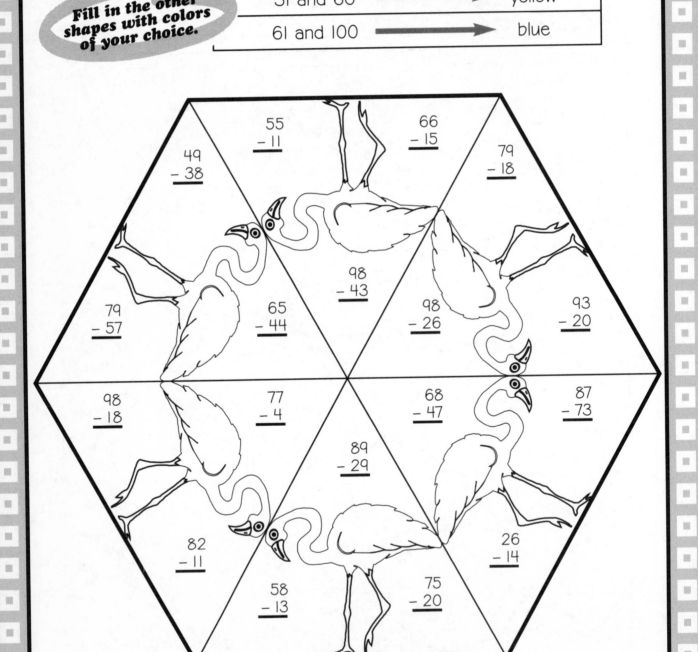

$$49 - 38$$

$$55 - 11$$

$$66 - 15$$

$$79 - 18$$

$$98 - 43$$

$$79 - 57$$

$$65 - 44$$

$$98 - 26$$

$$93 - 20$$

$$98 - 18$$

$$77 - 4$$

$$68 - 47$$

$$87 - 73$$

$$89 - 29$$

$$82 - 11$$

$$58 - 13$$

$$75 - 20$$

$$26 - 14$$

Name _____ **Date** _____

Joe saw a yo-yo in the store.

It cost 45¢.

He liked it, but he didn't have any money.

Then Joe found some money.

He found a quarter in his jeans' pocket.

He found a dime in his backpack.

He found a nickel in his shoe.

He found 7 pennies in his other pocket.

Can you help Joe count his money?

Answer the questions about the story.

1. How much money did Joe find in all? _____

2. Can he buy the yo-yo? _____

3. If Joe buys the yo-yo, will he have any money left over? _____

4. How much? _____

5. How many more cents would Joe need to make 50¢? _____

Name _____   **Date** _____

Read each clue. If the answer is no, make an **X** in the square.
If the answer is yes, make an **O** in the square.

Clues

1. Angela does not play Frisbee or football.
2. Kate plays only football.
3. Mark does not play football or basketball.

Which sport does each person play?

Angela plays

_____

Kate plays

_____

Mark plays

_____

	basketball	Frisbee	football
Angela			
Kate			
Mark			

Ask ten classmates which sport they like best. Use tally marks
to record each vote.

baseball _____   basketball _____   cycling _____

football _____   Frisbee _____   hockey _____

skating _____   soccer _____   swimming _____

The Substitute Teacher Resource Book • Scholastic Teaching Resources

Name _____ **Date** _____

Read each clue. If the answer is no, make an **X** in the square.
If the answer is yes, make an **O** in the square.

Clues

1. Lisa did not buy a bear, dog, or turtle.
2. Daniel bought a dog.
3. Maria does not like cats, dogs, or bears.
4. Bill bought a bear.

What did each person buy?

Daniel bought a _____ . Lisa bought a _____ .

Maria bought a _____ . Bill bought a _____ .

	bear	cat	dog	turtle
Daniel				
Lisa				
Maria				
Bill				

Name _____ **Date** _____

In the space below, draw a picture of your classroom and some of the people in it.

Your class is one of a kind! Tell about your class.

How many children are in your classroom? _____

How many teachers are in your classroom? _____

How many boys are in your classroom? _____

How many girls are in your classroom? _____

What is your favorite school activity? _____

What is the name of your school? _____

What is the name of your teacher? _____

Challenge! Are there more girls or boys in your class? Make a bar graph on a piece of graph paper or on the back of the page that shows how many boys and how many girls there are.

The Substitute Teacher Resource Book • Scholastic Teaching Resources

Poem adapted from "Flag Day" in *The Scholastic Big Book of Holidays Around the Year* by Susan Dillon (Scholastic, 2003),
The Substitute Teacher Resource Book • Scholastic Teaching Resources

Name _____ Date _____

Look at this drawing of the American flag. Color the spaces around the stars blue. Color the stars white. Now color the top stripe and the bottom stripe red. Skip a line and color every other stripe red.

Here's an American flag just for you.
Take out your markers, red, white, and blue.
The top box is blue, for the sky at night.
A star for each state, 50 shiny and white.
The stripes alternate red, white, red, white
For the 13 colonies and our independence fight.

Read the poem and answer these questions about our flag.

How many stars are on the flag? _____

Why do we have that number of stars? _____

How many stripes are on the flag? _____

Write the names of all three colors on the American flag.

_____ , _____ , and _____

Do you have an American flag in your classroom? _____

Do you know the words to the Pledge of Allegiance? _____

On the back of this page, draw a holiday or special time when you noticed the flag.

Name _____ **Date** _____

Did you know . . .

The Pilgrims put milk on their popcorn and ate it like we eat cereal.

Some American Indians ate hot popcorn in their soup.

No matter what color the popcorn is before it is popped, it is always white after it pops.

People found 1,000-year-old popcorn—It still popped!

There is a little bit of water inside each kernel of popcorn. When it gets hot, it explodes and pops the corn.

Tell one fact you know about popcorn:

Draw a picture and write a sentence to tell how and where you like to eat your popcorn.

Name _____ **Date** _____

Did you know that an octopus can change colors? The colors tell us what the octopus is feeling. If the octopus is brown, it is calm. If it turns white, this means it is frightened. Sometimes an octopus will turn red. What do you think this means? It means he is angry. When the octopus squirts out black ink, he is telling you to go away from him.

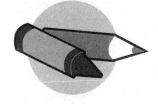

Color the octopi.
Be sure to match the color
to the feeling word.
Draw ink coming from
the angry octopus.

"Octopi" means more than one octopus.

This octopus is. . .   calm

This octopus is. . .   scared

This octopus is. . .   angry

Easy-to-Play Games and Quiet Activities

Look at me now!

Descriptive language

We often think that students by first and second grade have a pretty good grasp of language—exposure to descriptive language boosts their comprehension and vocabulary for reading and writing. This game engages children with the language of describing clothing and appearances.

To play the game, begin by asking, "Who can I look at? Who is wearing the color red?" Children wearing red must point to it, stand up and say, "Look at me now. I'm wearing red." Have those students sit down and then ask another question you know children will be able to answer. This may seem like a very simple game to adults, but almost every child gets to "win" and participate in this game—and in the meantime, they will actually increase their vocabularies.

Here are some more ideas for "Look at me now!" questions, which you can adapt to what you see in the classroom:

WHO CAN I LOOK AT? WHO HAS . . .

stripes	plaid	buttons	tie shoes
buckles	a part in their hair	a ribbon	lace
Velcro	a watch	letters	a ring
polka dots	a collar	long sleeves	jeans
shorts	leather shoes	short sleeves	a dress
hair barrette	a sweater	snaps	cuffs
braids	a pony tail	curly hair	
a cartoon character shirt	a sports team shirt	a school shirt	

HINT: *To make this game even more valuable, you can ask each child to say the name of the thing that has the characteristic. In the example for red, the student responses might be, "I have a red bow in my hair," "I have red shoe laces," "I have red buttons," "I have a red letter," or "I have red earrings." If the child doesn't know the name of the object containing red, say, "I can see John is wearing red sneakers."*

HINT: *Have students draw a self portrait (or a picture of their best friend or their family). Encourage them to add as many details as they can, such as color and patterns to their clothes, buttons or zippers, and favorite hats on their heads or barrettes in their hair. The more details they can use to describe, the more they are noticing about the physical character of a person. This is a great activity to celebrate individuality and to build characterization skills for story writing.*

The Substitute Teacher Resource Book • Scholastic Teaching Resources

The Name Game*

Memory/name recognition

Children love to play memory games. If they are beginning to recognize their own names and their classmates' in print, try this version of Concentration. Using large index cards or halves of 8 1/2″ x 11″ paper, write the name of every child in the class on two cards (or have the children write their own names twice). Use sticky tack or tape to set all the names face down on the chalkboard or wall where the children can see them. Let each child or pair of children take a turn, selecting two cards to see if they match. If they do, turn the cards that remain face up. If they don't, the child or pair places the cards face down again, and the next child or pair takes a turn. Play continues until all matches have been found. Variations include making matching cards of each child's name and his or her last name or the child's name and that of his or her favorite meal.

*Adapted from *Classroom Routines That Really Work for Pre-K and Kindergarten* by Kathleen Hayes and Reneé Creange (Scholastic, 2001)

"Simon Says" Math*

Math skills/physical coordination

As in the traditional game Simon Says, the leader asks players to perform tasks involving addition and subtraction (or simple counting skills for younger students). Choose a leader. Have all students stand in an area where they can move about freely. For each round, the leader makes three choices: (1) whether to say "Simon says" or nothing at all, (2) an easy physical activity students can repeat such as clapping, jumping jacks, or turning in a circle and (3) an addition or subtraction problem or counting challenge that students can solve. The leader makes a three-part statement such as, "Simon says jump the sum of 3 plus 2" or "Clap your hands 4 minus 3 times." Players must immediately decide to carry out the action or stay still if they did not hear the command, "Simon says." Players remain in the game if they performed the action correctly or did not move when a direction was given without the "Simon says" command. You and the leader may ask players to sit aside when they have performed the action without the "Simon says" command or performed the action incorrectly. You might want players who sit out to help make sure students remaining perform their actions correctly.

HINT: *If students need extra support, write entire statements on index cards. The leader then needs only to pick a card from the deck, read it to the group, and help determine who remains in the game and who drops out. For nonreading groups, you can be the leader.*

*Adapted from *Mega-Fun Math Games* by Michael Schiro (Scholastic, 1995)

Reading or Math Flashcard Fun

A really good way to do flashcard practice is to line the students up in two teams that have an unequal number of students. The two students in front of the line advance and are given a math problem or a word to read. Whoever is the first to answer correctly earns a point for his or her team. Simply lay the card down to your right or your left—on the side of the team that earned the point. Both students then go to the end of the line. Because the two lines are uneven, students come up against a different person each time they are challenged.

To find the winner, simply count the number of cards in each pile.

Make this easier by not putting down the card until the next two students are up. That keeps the next problem hidden and reveals it at the same time for both students.

Spelling Bee Fun for Youngsters

Spelling From Memory
Conduct a spelling bee using words from the first units in the student basal speller or from the list on page 93. Follow the format for a traditional spelling bee. Then try some of the alternative ways to conduct spelling practice.

Traditional
All students stand in a line around the classroom. Start at one end and give out a spelling word. The child says the word, spells it and says the word again. If the word is spelled correctly, go to the next child and present a new word. If the word is missed, that same word is given to the next child. No one sits down or is "out" of the game.

Note: Some kids will miss on purpose to *try* to get out of the game and get to sit out. Don't give them that opportunity to get out of spelling practice. If you find that you have a wide range of spelling ability in the classroom, this method may be embarrassing for the poorer spellers. Switch to one of the alternative spelling bees outlined below and on page 93.

Alternative Spelling Bees
Paper Bee: This version works well if children have a difficult time behaving, or if you feel that in some may be embarrassed about their spelling skills. Have students fold a standard sheet of notebook paper in half five times (when the paper is unfolded it will have 32 little boxes). Have children write each new word you call in a new box. The papers can be scored individually or the total number of correct responses can be added to get a team score.

HINT: *If you give prizes for this game, try giving them to anyone who scores above a certain number correct. For example, if you used 32 words, anyone that got more than 20 correct could get a prize. Always try to avoid embarrassing any child in the class.*

HINT: *Stickers from your tote bag make great prizes. If you are out of these, write "Great Speller" on a stick-on name tag and give these to children to wear to lunch or home to show their families. You can also use yellow and black markers to draw a giant bee on the paper spelling bee pages. The bee can have a speech bubble saying "BEE-utiful spelling!"*

Spelling Bee Hive: Another alternative is to have a spelling bee hive. In this case, children are divided into groups of 3, 4, or 5. A word is given to the group. Group members discuss how to spell the word and then one child spells it out loud. Then a word is given to the next group. Each time the group gets a turn, children take turns being the speller. You can also divide the chalkboard into sections and let the child write the word in a column for his or her team after the short group discussion. Many students find writing the word easier than spelling it out loud.

GRADE 1 WORD LIST

Am	as	and	are	as	at	ate	be	black
blue	book	boy	by	came	can	car	come	day
did	do	don't	down	eat	eight	fast	farther	five
for	four	friend	from	gave	get	girl	give	go
goes	good	got	green	had	has	have	he	if
in	is	it	jump	little	look	me	mother	my
new	night	nine	no	not	of	off	old	on
one	orange	out	play	rain	ran	red	run	sat
saw	see	sever	she	sit	six	stop	ten	that
the	they	this	three	to	two	up	want	was
we	went	were	will	with	yellow	yes	you	

GRADE 2 WORD LIST

After	all	any	ask	before	best	better	both	brother
brown	but	child	children	cold	drink	drank	early	end
every	fall	fell	few	first	Friday	funny	goodbye	hello
help	her	here	hers	him	his	how	into	keep
kept	large	long	made	make	man	many	men	Monday
more	myself	none	now	open	out	over	please	pretty
purple	quiet	read	said	sang	Saturday	say	school	second
short	sing	sister	sleep	slept	small	some	soon	
spring	story	summer	Sunday	take				
thank	their	them	then	there				
third	Thursday	took	town					
Tuesday	under	us	Wednesday					
what	when	where	white					
who	why	wide	winter					
woman	women	your						

TIP

These lists appear in *100 Words Kids Need to Read by First Grade* and *100 Words Kids Need to Read by Second Grade* (Scholastic, 2002)—a great resource for your tote bag!

Favorite Activities Tracking Chart

As you travel from classroom to classroom, you may find it difficult to remember which activities you have used with particular groups. Keep track of your favorite activities (and add ideas for modifications) by filling in this chart after you complete each assignment.

Activity	Date/ School	Grade/ Class	Comments *(e.g., level of difficulty, how students responded, how to model, ways to group students, time allotment, and so on.)*